Through
Temple
Doors

Through Temple Doors

John K. Edmunds

Bookcraft
Salt Lake City, Utah

Library of Congress Catalog Card Number: 78-61502
ISBN 0-88494-348-8

8 9 10   89 88 87 86 85 84

Lithographed in the United States of America
PUBLISHERS PRESS
Salt Lake City, Utah

To Jasmine

CONTENTS

Contents

INTRODUCTION

I stood at the window of our home high up on the avenues and looked out over the Salt Lake Valley. It was early morning, and, except for street lights and the signs on a few tall buildings, most of the valley lay in darkness.

The most noticeable exception to dark buildings was the temple with its six brilliantly lighted towers. It stood out like a diamond set among the high buildings that now surround and dwarf it in size.

I thought of the stone steps laid in the circular stairways leading from the basement to the top floor in the four corners of the building, each step weighing about seventeen hundred pounds, all crafted by hand and with such care and precision that there is not room for a knife blade to be inserted between the stones at any place. The building is unmatched in beauty of design and craftsmanship both inside and outside. It was built by men who, in many cases, lacked adequate housing for their families. It was built in their poverty, but they were building a house for their God, and they built it with faith and with care.

Yes, to me it was the most beautiful building in all the world. Then for a brief moment a sadness came over me. I found myself wishing there were no building higher than the temple, that it might have a superior height consonant with its superior importance. No building can excel the temple in importance, I said to myself, then why should those tall buildings dwarf it in height?

It is the house of God, where the final ordinances and instructions for the exaltation of the living and all the necessary ordinances for the dead are bestowed. I would soon be down there, instructing the men who come for their sacred endowment and the grooms coming for instruction and the holy ordinance of marriage in the new and everlasting covenant, which could be received only in the temple.

I thought of the many times when I had stood in a sealing room with a thrill in my soul and tears in my eyes as I looked upon a clean, worthy young couple kneeling at the altar with tears in their eyes as I pronounced them "husband and wife for time and for all eternity." I thought of the Spirit of God bearing witness to my spirit that the ordinance was divine and that the power and authority conferred upon me by God, through his prophet, to seal on earth and in heaven, is a reality.

My thoughts turned to the neatly groomed group of missionaries, about two hundred and fifty young men and women, together with older couples, who would enter the temple this morning, and then dressed in white would receive their own important endowment or receive this great blessing for and in behalf of the dead. In the hour interval between their two endowment sessions, they would gather in the solemn assembly room—the room where the Saints assembled on April 6, 1893, for the dedicating of the house of the Lord. There they would ask questions concerning the temple, its principles and ordinances. It would be my privilege today to respond to their questions. From the temple, endowed with knowledge and "power from on high," these missionaries would go forth into the world to bring hundreds and thousands of honest seekers for truth into the Church and kingdom of God.

Marvelous as this conversion accomplishment might be, it would probably pale into lesser significance when compared with the conversion taking place in paradise, where billions of our Father's children who departed this life without the privilege of receiving the gospel in mortality, were being taught by the great prophets and faithful elders of this and former dispensations. The thought occurred to me that all these converts, on both sides of the veil, would be greatly limited in the fruits of their conversion but for the blessings of the temple. And, looking thoughtfully upon the temple, I said, "That's where the action is!"

My mind turned to an introduction I was given a few days before as I responded to an invitation to address a large body of University of Utah students met in an institute assembly. "John K. Edmunds," said the man making the introduction, "is the president of the Salt Lake Temple; he is the Steward of the House of Jesus Christ."

I won't soon forget the impact of that introduction upon me. Could it be that I, who such a short few years ago had been a farm boy down in Sanpete Valley and had herded sheep in the mountains overlooking the little Utah town which had been named "Wales" by its humble but proud Welsh founders, should now be introduced as "Steward of the House of Jesus Christ"?

I could hardly give credence to the thought. But still, I knew that I had been called and set apart to preside in that house, and I believed it to be the house envisioned by the prophets Isaiah and Micah who, centuries before the earthly advent of Jesus Christ, the God of Jacob, had prophesied:

> And it shall come to pass in the last days, that the mountain of the Lord's house shall be established in the top of the mountains, and shall be exalted above the hills; and all nations shall flow unto it.
>
> And many people shall go and say, Come ye, and let us go up to the mountain of the Lord, to the house of the God of Jacob; and he will teach us of his ways, and we will walk in his paths: for out of Zion shall go forth the law, and the word of the Lord from Jerusalem.[1]

I looked at my watch. There was no time now for being lost in thought: dawn had come; a pink and gold tint was beginning to show over the eastern mountains. I left the window, and a few minutes later Sister Edmunds—the temple matron—and I were immersed in the joyous activities of the "house of the Lord."

NOTES

1. Isaiah 2:2-3; see also Micah 4:1-2.

1

HOUSES OF
THE LORD

Among all the churches and sects comprising what is known as Christianity, The Church of Jesus Christ of Latter-day Saints stands uniquely alone in its adherence to the teachings and practices within the scope of temple administration.

We build our meetinghouses and places of public gathering much as others erect their chapels, churches, cathedrals, and synagogues. But unlike any of these buildings is the temple with its eternal objectives, its distinct history, and its divine purposes.

What is a temple? By derivation, the English term *temple* comes from the Latin *templum,* and is the equivalent of the Hebrew term *beth-elohim* (sometimes contracted as *beth-el*), meaning the "House of God," and each of the Mormon temples dotting the world rightfully bears the solemn inscription: *"The House of the Lord."*

Throughout the ages of the world the temples of God have been built by his revelation and commandment. God has not only made known the place and time of their erection but he, himself, has been the architect of his houses. From the beginning of their exodus, the children of Israel provided a place of abode for their God. The first of these was a sacred tent called the "tabernacle of the congregation,"[1] which was pitched outside the camp of Israel and into which Moses went to commune with God. Moses tells us that in this tabernacle God spake unto him "face to face, as a man speaketh unto his friend."[2] The honor of God's presence within it made it a "temple."

The tabernacle of the congregation was superseded by a tabernacle built at the foot of Mount Sinai pursuant to the commandment of God, who was the sole architect of this portable sanctuary that consisted of a wooden framework, rectangular in shape, and covered with curtains. By commandment Moses left the camp of Israel and went up into Mount Sinai for instructional conferences with God, the first of these conferences lasting forty days. During this conference, the exact pattern of the sanctuary, with its appointments and "instruments," was shown him. God said unto Moses:

> Speak unto the children of Israel, that they bring me an offering: of every man that giveth it willingly with his heart ye shall take my offering. . . .
> And let them make me a sanctuary; that I may dwell among them.
> According to all that I shew thee, after the pattern of the tabernacle, and the pattern of all the instruments thereof, even so shall ye make it.[3]

The scriptural record confirms that

> According to all that the Lord commanded Moses, so the children of Israel made all the work.
> And Moses did look upon all the work, and, behold, they had done it as the Lord had commanded, even so had they done it: and Moses blessed them.[4]

Parenthetically, we must not close our eyes to the significant principle in giving involved in these instructions of God to Moses. While God called for the offerings of his people to build a sanctuary for him, only offerings given willingly of the heart were acceptable to him. The prophet Moroni elaborates on this principle by saying that "if a man . . . giveth a gift . . . grudgingly . . . it is counted unto him the same as if he had retained the gift; wherefore he is counted evil before God."[5] This lesson must not be lost on

Latter-day Saints. In our tithes and offerings and in all our contributions to the cause and work of God—and the principle applies to time and talents as well as to material means—we should learn and remember that only that which is given willingly of the heart is acceptable to God and will call forth his blessings upon us.

From the time the children of Israel left Sinai, during the wanderings of their exodus until their entrance into the land of Canaan—their promised land—they carried their portable sanctuary with them as a place of worship and a holy dwelling-place for their God. The biblical record states that

> The glory of the Lord filled the tabernacle. . . .
> For the cloud of the Lord was upon the tabernacle by day, and fire was on it by night, in the sight of all the house of Israel, throughout all their journeys.[6]

This supernatural phenomenon of the pillar of a cloud by day and the pillar of fire by night, referred to as the "Shekenah," was evidence enough that the sacred sanctuary was the dwelling-place of Jehovah and, therefore, the children of Israel referred to it as their "temple."[7]

When the children of Israel had established themselves in their promised land, Hiram, King of Tyre, sought for an alliance of peace and friendship with Israel, and David— King of all Israel—formed an alliance with him. As an evidence of this friendship, Hiram sent cedar-timber from Lebanon, with masons and carpenters to build a palace for David.[8] David accepted the palace, but his enjoyment of it was marred by a troubled thought, which he expressed to his chief adviser, the prophet Nathan:

> Lo, I dwell in an house of cedars, but the ark of the covenant of the Lord remaineth under curtains.[9]

The ark of the covenant was a sacred chest, about forty-five inches in length and twenty-seven inches in width and height. It is said to have been made of "shittim-wood, overlaid with pure gold, and had a golden mitre round the top. . . . The cover of the ark was a plate of pure gold, overshadowed by two cherubim [angels], with their faces bent down and their wings meeting. This was the very throne of

Jehovah. . . . It was called the *mercy-seat* or *propitiatory*, because Jehovah there revealed himself, especially on the great Day of Atonement, as 'God pardoning iniquity, transgression, and sin.' "[10] The ark contained, among other things, the two tables of stone on which were inscribed the Ten Commandments and was housed within the tabernacle compartment known as the "Holy of Holies." It was the only object in this sacred place.

David told the prophet Nathan of his desire and intention to build a permanent temple as a dwelling-place for the Lord and provide for the ark of the covenant a more suitable place than a portable tent. Without seeking to know the will of God concerning the matter, Nathan gave his blessing and approval to the venture. However, that same night the word of God came to Nathan, commanding him to tell David that he was not to build a house for God to dwell in and also reminding him that he, the Lord, had been content to dwell in a tent from the beginning of the Exodus.[11]

David had been a man of war and had shed much blood, and in at least one instance it had been innocent blood—the blood of Uriah. Therefore, God could not accept a house built by him. However, the building of a temple to God was not permanently prohibited; it was simply postponed, pending the accession to the throne of Israel of a king better suited to the building of the house of the Lord. While David made vast preparations for the building of a house for God, it was not his blessing to build the house. David was told by God, through his prophet, Nathan, that one of his sons would build the temple and that it would be built in a place chosen by God himself. This blessing fell to Solomon.

Upon the death of David and the accession of Solomon, his son, to the throne of Israel, Solomon sent a message to Hiram, King of Tyre, which said:

> As thou didst deal with David my father, and didst send him cedars to build him an house to dwell therein, even so deal with me.
>
> Behold, I build an house to the name of the Lord my God, to dedicate it to him. . . .
>
> And the house which I build is great: for great is our God above all gods.

But who is able to build him an house, seeing the heaven and heaven of heavens cannot contain him? who am I, then, that I should build him an house, save only to burn sacrifice before him?

Send me now therefore a man cunning to work in gold, and in silver, and in brass, and in iron, and in purple, and crimson, and blue, and that can skill to grave with the cunning men that are with me in Judah and in Jerusalem, whom David my father did provide.

Send me also cedar trees, fir trees, and algum trees, out of Lebanon: for I know that thy servants can skill to cut timber in Lebanon; and behold, my servants shall be with thy servants,

Even to prepare me timber in abundance: for the house which I am about to build shall be wonderful great.[12]

By return letter, King Hiram gladly promised the requested assistance. An arrangement was made between Solomon and Hiram by which Hiram gave cedar and fir trees out of Lebanon, which his servants felled, and which the servants of Solomon squared and fitted together for their places in the temple. All of this preparatory work was done in Tyre, before shipment to Jerusalem. The finished timber, together with the great stones for the foundation of the temple, all finished and ready for assembly, were floated to Joppa under the care of the Tyrian sailors. From Joppa the servants of Solomon undertook the thirty-mile transport by land to Jerusalem.

Besides these contributions of labor and materials, it is recorded history "that Hiram [Huram] supplied Solomon with a chief architect, a namesake of his own, for whom the King of Tyre expressed the reverence of a disciple for an artist by calling him 'Hiram, my father.' "[13]

The erection of the temple in Jerusalem was begun during the fourth year of the reign of Solomon and was completed in seven and a half years (1,012 to 1,005 B.C.). One hundred and eighty thousand workers and three thousand six hundred supervisors or overseers were employed in the monumental task. However, "so complete were the preparations [made in Tyre] that no sound of axe or hammer was heard about the building during its whole erection—'Like some tall palm, the noiseless fabric grew.' "[14]

While Hiram, the son of a daughter of the tribe of Dan and of a Tyrian artist, is referred to as the chief architect of the temple, in reality its chief architect was God himself, whose house it was. Like the tabernacle built at Sinai, the temple consisted of three parts—the porch, the Holy Place, and the Holy of Holies. In this, and all essential points, the temple was modeled after the tabernacle. The temple proper, in all its dimensions, was exactly double that of the tabernacle, which was built by Moses according to the pattern, design, and specifications prescribed by God, its architect. The chief difference between the tabernacle and the temple was that the temple had chambers built about the sanctuary for the abode of priests and attendants and for storage purposes and was constructed of the most precious and costly materials.

The grandeur and fame of the magnificent structure known as the "Temple of Solomon" spread throughout the world, and all Israel assembled at Jerusalem for its dedication.

On the day of dedication, the ark of the covenant was brought to its place in the Holy of Holies. Then God signified his coming to accept and take possession of his house by causing a cloud to fill it. This manifestation of God's approval of the sanctuary was so glorious that the priests were unable to stand on their feet to minister therein. The scriptural record simply says: "The glory of the Lord had filled the house of the Lord."[15]

When succeeding generations of Israel transgressed the laws of God and thus withdrew from him, God ceased to acknowledge this sanctuary as his, and the costly structure was plundered, defiled, and eventually destroyed.

Years later, on the site where the Temple of Solomon had stood, a repentant Israel erected another temple, with the aid and under the aegis of the Persian kings, Cyrus and Darius. This temple, known as the Temple of Zerubbabel (after the head of the tribe of Judah, who had it built), was completed in 515 B.C. and stood for about five hundred years before falling into virtual ruin and disuse.

When Herod I, better known as Herod the Great, came

to the throne, he undertook the reconstruction and expansion of the Temple of Zerubbabel to satisfy his own ulterior purposes and to win the friendship of the Jews. The Jews, however, were not willing to trust Herod and considered him unworthy to rebuild the temple. Therefore, the priests themselves built the temple proper. But the cloisters, outer enclosures, and other buildings were added by Herod.

The reconstruction began about 16 B.C. and was still in progress during the lifetime of Christ. This last temple in Jerusalem, known as the "Temple of Herod"—a most unholy and unsuitable name for the sanctuary into which Jesus was wont to go and which he referred to as "my house"[16]— had hardly reached completion when the crucifixion occurred.

At the death of Jesus "the veil of the temple was rent in twain from the top to the bottom"[17] by an unseen power. The veil of the temple was a sumptuous curtain that separated the Holy Place from the Holy of Holies. Dr. William Smith, in his *Old Testament History* says:—

> It was called the VEIL, as it hid from the eyes of all but the high-priest the inmost sanctuary, where Jehovah dwelt on his mercy-seat. . . .
> Hence, "to enter within the veil" is to have the closest access to God.[18]

With the rending of the veil, the Mosaic dispensation came to an end. Not long thereafter, God withdrew his protection from the temple and from those who unrighteously ministered therein. In A.D. 70 it was so utterly destroyed by the Roman legions under Titus that, as Jesus had predicted, not one stone was left upon another; and to this day, except for the abortive attempt of the Roman Emperor Julian in the fourth century,[19] no effort has been made to restore or rebuild it.

It must not be assumed, because history has placed a lid of silence on the subject, that temple building originated with the Israelites only after their deliverance from Egyptian bondage. The rites and ordinances of animal sacrifice and baptism, which were major, integral functions of the Israelite temples, are as old as the human race. The first recorded commandment given to Adam and Eve after their expulsion from the Garden of Eden was to "worship the Lord their God, and . . . offer the firstlings of their flocks, for an offering unto the Lord."[20] Some time thereafter, an angel explained to Adam that this animal sacrificial offering was "a similitude of the sacrifice of the Only Begotten of the Father, which is full of grace and truth."[21]

The ecclesiastical historian, Eusebius, whose life spanned the latter part of the third and the early part of the fourth centuries after Christ, has made some strikingly interesting observations concerning the beginnings of Christianity. He writes:

> Although we certainly are a youthful people and this undeniably new name of Christians has only lately become known among all nations, nevertheless our life and mode of conduct, together with our religious principles, have not been recently invented by us, but from almost the beginnings of man were built on the natural concepts of those whom God loved in the distant past. . . . It is obvious that they knew God's Christ Himself, since He appeared to Abraham, instructed Isaac, spoke to Israel, and conversed freely with Moses and the prophets who came later, as I have already shown. . . .
>
> Obviously we must regard the religion proclaimed in recent years to all nations through Christ's teaching as none other than the first, most ancient, and most primitive of all religions, discovered by Abraham and his followers, God's beloved.[22]

The ordinance of baptism was explained and administered to Adam as part of the "plan of salvation unto all men," through the blood of the Only Begotten Son of God who should "come in the meridian of time."[23] If the gospel of Jesus Christ and the ordinances thereof were here from the beginning, is it improbable that temples, in which the ordinances were administered, existed also?

There is ample evidence that the Jews erected and maintained temples other than those which were built in Jerusalem. The eminent Jewish historian, Josephus, records in his "Antiquities of the Jews" that Onias, son of a Jewish high priest, of the same name, wrote an epistle to Ptolemy and Cleopatra, King and Queen of Egypt, requesting their approval for his building a temple to Almighty God in Egypt and informing them that the prophet Isaiah who lived about six hundred years earlier had foretold that such a temple should be built. They responded with an epistle in these words:

> King Ptolemy and Queen Cleopatra to Onias, send greeting. We have read thy petition, wherein thou desirest leave to be given to thee to purge that temple which is fallen down at Leontopolis, in the Nomus of Heliopolis, and which is named from the country Bubastis; on which account we cannot but wonder that it should be pleasing to God to have a temple erected in a place so unclean, and so full of sacred animals. But since thou sayest that Isaiah the prophet foretold this long ago, we give thee leave to do it, if it may be done according to your law, and so that we may not appear to have at all offended God herein.[24]

Josephus goes on to record:

> So Onias took the place, and built a temple, and an altar to God, like indeed to that at Jerusalem, but smaller and poorer. I do not think it proper for me now to describe its dimensions, or its vessels, which have been already described in my seventh book of the Wars of the Jews. However, Onias found other Jews like himself, together with priests and Levites, that there performed divine service.[25]

The branches of Israel that had been established on what is now known as the American continent prior to the birth of Christ, built temples "after the manner of the temple of Solomon"[26] and performed the prescribed Mosaic rites and ordinances therein; but the records of these peoples shed no light upon the changes in temple rites, ordinances, and uses following the atonement of Christ.

While the Israelites viewed their temples as sanctuaries where Jehovah might come and dwell and commune with his people, these sacred buildings were primarily constructed for and devoted to solemn rites and ceremonies that had been prescribed by Jehovah, including various sacrificial offerings that were the prototypes of the sacrificial atonement for sin to be made by the Lord himself in the meridian of time.

I am sure it would be quite possible to reproduce the physical Temple of Solomon from the biblical record alone, but the biblical record has little to offer with respect to the necessary changes in temple ordinances and ministration brought about by the completion of Christ's sacrificial atonement, since the temple was destroyed at the approximate time of the close of the biblical record.

Since the Mosaic rites and ordinances involving animal sacrifice associated with pre-Christian temples were fulfilled in Christ's sacrificial death, the question arises as to what use future temples would be devoted. What rites and ordinances would God ordain to be performed therein? It is generally recognized that upon the death of the last of Christ's apostles, revelation ceased and the heavens were closed. With no prophet or apostle to whom God might communicate new temple rites, ordinances, and uses, and no temple in which such rites and ordinances could be performed, temple ministration came to an end on the Eastern continent shortly after the time of Christ.

In view of this lack of scriptural instruction in the records of Christ's day, the only source from which we could draw the knowledge of doctrines, ordinances, rites, and ceremonies to be taught and practiced in our present temples would be *revelation from God*; he alone can give to man the authority and power to make those rites and ordinances effective beyond the grave, for such authority and power is superior to any that earthly legislators could originate or enact.

Seventeen centuries after the final destruction of the temple in which Christ ministered among the Jews, the Lord again raised up a prophet and once more called upon his people to build for him a house in which the sacred ordinances of the gospel could be administered. His first call upon the Church to build a temple came by revelation to the Prophet Joseph Smith in December, 1830, in which he said: "I am Jesus Christ, the Son of God; wherefore, gird up your loins and I will suddenly come to my temple."[27] By subsequent revelation, the site, inner dimensions, and nature of the sanctuary were made known, and the first of all the temples to be built in this final dispensation was erected at Kirtland, Ohio. The Lord said to Joseph Smith:

> Here is wisdom, and the mind of the Lord—let the house be built; not after the manner of the world . . . let it be built after the manner which I shall show unto three of you, whom ye shall appoint and ordain unto this power.[28]

Pursuant to this revelation, a committee of three— Hyrum Smith, Reynolds Cahoon, and Jared Carter—was appointed, to whom the plans for the house of the Lord were shown. You will note that here again, as in the days of Moses and Solomon, God was the architect of his house.

Though it was not the magnificent structure that marked the Temple of Solomon and certain of the temples subsequently erected in this last dispensation, it was the best that an impoverished people could offer as a house for their God. While the men of the Church were devoting their time and skills, which was all that many of them had to offer, self-sacrificing women were grinding their precious china into fine pieces to be mixed into the external wall-coating to give luster and beauty to the house of the Lord.

The Lord accepted their humble offering when, on a Sabbath afternoon one week after the formal dedication of the sanctuary and in fulfillment of his promise, he suddenly came to his temple. A meeting of the Church was being held in the sacred building.

The Prophet Joseph Smith and his counselor, Oliver Cowdery, received the sacrament from the Twelve Apostles and proceeded to the pulpit. The veils which divided the sanctuary into compartments were lowered and the Prophet and his counselor, now out of the sight of the congregation, bowed themselves in "solemn and silent prayer."[29] Soon, a glorious vision, or series of visions, came to them. Here is their record of this sublime experience:

> The veil was taken from our minds, and the eyes of our understanding were opened.
> We saw the Lord standing upon the breastwork of the pulpit, before us; and under his feet was a paved work of pure gold, in color like amber.

15

His eyes were as a flame of fire; the hair of his head was white like the pure snow; his countenance shone above the brightness of the sun; and his voice was as the sound of the rushing of great waters, even the voice of Jehovah, saying:

I am the first and the last; I am he who liveth, I am he who was slain; I am your advocate with the Father. . . .

Let the hearts of your brethren rejoice, and let the hearts of all my people rejoice, who have, with their might, built this house to my name.

For behold, I have accepted this house, and my name shall be here; and I will manifest myself to my people in mercy in this house. . . .

Yea, the hearts of thousands and tens of thousands shall greatly rejoice in consequence of the blessings which shall be poured out. . . .

And the fame of this house shall spread to foreign lands; and this is the beginning of the blessings which shall be poured out upon the heads of my people. Even so. Amen.[30]

What were the blessings and endowments to be poured out in this sanctuary in consequence of which "the hearts of thousands and tens of thousands shall greatly rejoice"? They were endowments of knowledge pertaining to the ceremonies, rites, and ordinances of the temple following the sacrificial atonement of Jesus Christ, the atonement being the pivot between the sacrifices of Israel's temples before Christ and the rites, ceremonies, and ordinances of the temples of today. They were also endowments of priesthood power and authority to officiate in all the ordinances, ceremonies, and endowments of priesthood keys to direct and proceed with the work to be carried on in these holy sanctuaries for and in behalf of the living and the dead.

Having fulfilled its divine purpose, the Kirtland Temple was superseded by the Nauvoo Temple, the site and nature of which were revealed by the Lord to the Prophet Joseph Smith. Hardly had the temple been completed and endowments received in it by the living, when the Saints were driven from Illinois, and the temple was left to the enemies of the Church, to be defiled and eventually destroyed.

During the long, hard journey from Illinois to the valleys of the Rocky Mountains, the Saints were dreaming of and discussing the building of another temple to their God—a temple envisioned by Isaiah and Micah long before the birth of Christ—the house of the God of Jacob, which was to be established in the top of the mountains, to which people of all nations should flow.

As with ancient Israel, God had chosen the place for his modern Israel to settle and also the site for his house. Upon his entrance into the Salt Lake Valley, Brigham Young recognized God's chosen place for the settlement of the Saints because of an earlier vision he had been given in Nauvoo. Years later this vision was described by Elder Erastus Snow. In an address which he delivered on July 25, 1880, in Salt Lake City, he said:

> Brother Woodruff informed the people yesterday . . . how President Young as he emerged from the mouth of Emigration [Canyon], lifted himself up in his bed and peered out of his wagon which overlooked the valley, the cottonwoods on the creek, and the camp on the east side of the creek in fair view, and . . . said then, and afterwards to all the camp, *that this was the place he had seen long since in vision;* it was here he had seen the tent settling down from heaven and resting, and a voice said unto him: "Here is the place where my people Israel shall pitch their tents."[31]

Late in the afternoon of July 28, 1847, four days after the arrival of the Saints in the Salt Lake Valley, President Brigham Young, accompanied by Elders Heber C. Kimball, Willard Richards, Orson Pratt, Wilford Woodruff, George A. Smith, Amasa Lyman, Ezra T. Benson—all of whom were apostles—and Thomas Bullock, the president's secretary, made an exploratory trip in the valley. Wilford Woodruff wrote of this event:

> We walked from the north camp to about the center between the two creeks [forks of City Creek], when President Young waved his hands and said, "Here is the forty acres for the temple . . . and the city can be laid out perfectly square north and south, east and west."[32]

Planting his walking stick at a certain spot within the forty acres, President Young exclaimed, "Here we will build the Temple of our God." His daughter, Susa Young Gates, in collaboration with Leah D. Widtsoe, records that "Elder Woodruff drove a stake into the small hole made by that cane point and there to-day stands that 'frozen poem,' the Salt Lake Temple."[33]

His daughter's record continues: "Brigham Young then and always refused to take any credit for his share of this mammoth undertaking. 'I do not wish men to understand I had anything to do with our being moved here,' he said. 'That was the providence of the Almighty. It was the power of God that wrought out salvation for His people. I never could have devised such a scheme.' "[34]

The temple site was dedicated, and the ground was broken for the foundation on February 14, 1853. A few weeks later, on the sixth day of April, the cornerstones of the great temple were laid. The early leaders of the Church had by divine vision viewed the Salt Lake Temple in a spiritual form before the laying of those cornerstones.

On the day the cornerstones were laid, President Young, speaking in the Tabernacle, made these stirring statements to the Church in annual conference assembled:

> This I do know—there should be a Temple built here. . . .
> Now, some will want to know what kind of building it will
> be. . . . I know what it will be. I am not a visionary man,
> neither am I given much to prophesying. When I want any of
> that done I call on Brother Heber—he is my Prophet, he loves
> to prophesy, and I love to hear him. I scarcely ever say much
> about revelations, or visions, but suffice it to say, five years
> ago last July I was here, and saw in the Spirit the Temple not
> ten feet from where we have laid the Chief Corner Stone. I
> have not inquired what kind of a Temple we should build.
> Why? Because it was represented before me. I have never
> looked upon that ground, but the vision of it was there. I see
> it as plainly as if it was in reality before me.[35]

Before the laying of the cornerstones, there was much discussion as to the materials out of which the temple should be constructed. Some of the brethren suggested brick, others red sandstone, others adobe, and still others oolite.

Wilford Woodruff, the prophet whom God had chosen to dedicate the Salt Lake Temple, had beheld the temple in vision before the Saints' famous trek westward. He said:

> When in the western country, many years ago, before we
> came to the Rocky Mountains, I had a dream. I dreamed of

being in these mountains, and of seeing a large fine looking temple erected in one of these valleys which was built of cut granite stone. I saw that temple dedicated, and I attended the dedicatory services, and I saw a good many men that are living to-day in the midst of this people. . . . When the foundation of that temple was laid I thought of my dream. And whenever President Young held a council of the brethren of the Twelve and talked of building the temple of adobe or brick . . . I would say to myself, 'No, you will never do it;' because I had seen it in my dream built of some other material.[36]

Elder James E. Talmage gives this interesting account of how the question of the building material for the main structure of the temple was settled. He says:

At the forenoon session of the conference on October 9, 1852, President Heber C. Kimball submitted the question: "Shall we have the Temple built of stone from Red Butte, adobes, rock, or the best stone the mountains afford?" In reply, a resolution was adopted by unanimous vote to the effect "that we build a Temple of the best materials that can be obtained in the mountains of North America, and that the Presidency dictate where the stone and other materials shall be obtained." . . .

This modern House of the Lord was to be no temporary structure, nor of small proportions, nor of poor material, nor of mean or inadequate design. It was known at the outset that the building could not be finished for many a long year, for decades, perhaps. . . . The Temple was to be worthy of the great future. Sandstone, oolite, adobe blocks, each and all were considered, and in turn rejected. The decision was to this effect—the walls should be built of solid granite. An enormous deposit of this durable stone had been discovered in the Cottonwood canyons, twenty miles to the south-east, and to those faith-impelled people it was enough to know that suitable material was available.[37]

The building of the Salt Lake Temple must have been of extreme importance not only to the then living Latter-day Saints, but also to those laboring in the spirit world. Elder Parley P. Pratt testified that he beheld the Prophet Joseph Smith at the laying of the temple cornerstones on Wednesday, April 6, 1853. He stated in conference, the following day:

> Shall I speak my feelings, that I had on yesterday, while we were laying those Corner Stones of the Temple? Yes, I will utter them, if I can. It was not with my eyes, not with the power of actual vision, but . . . by the power of the Spirit, that it appeared to me that Joseph Smith, and his associate spirits, the Latter-day Saints, hovered above us on the brink of that foundation, and with them all the angels and spirits from the other world, that might be permitted. . . .[38]

As was expected, decades were required for the construction of the great temple. Exactly forty years from the date on which the cornerstones were laid, the Saints gathered in the large assembly room of the Salt Lake Temple for the dedication of this house of the Lord.

To prepare the Saints for the dedication, the First Presidency, on March 18, 1893, sent out a lengthy letter addressed "To the Officers and Members of the Church of Jesus Christ of Latter-day Saints." The first two paragraphs follow:

> The near approach of the date for the dedication of the Temple of our God moves us to express with some degree of fulness our feelings to our brethren, the officers of the Church, who with us bear the Priesthood of the Son of God, and to the Latter-day Saints generally; to the end that in entering that holy building we may all be found acceptable ourselves, with our households, and that the building which we shall dedicate may also be acceptable unto the Lord.
>
> The Latter-day Saints have used their means freely to erect other Temples in these valleys, and our Father has blessed us in our efforts. Today we enjoy the great happiness of having three of these sacred structures completed, dedicated to and accepted of the Lord, wherein the Saints can enter and attend to those ordinances which He, in His infinite goodness and kindness, has revealed. But for forty years the hopes, desires, and anticipations of the entire Church have been centered upon the completion of this edifice in the principal city of Zion. Its foundation was laid in the early days of our settlement in these mountains; and from that day until the present, the eyes of the members of the Church in every land have been lovingly directed toward it. Looking upon it as the Temple of temples, the people during all these years have labored with unceasing toil, undiminished patience, and ungrudging expenditure of means to bring it to its present condition of completion; and now that the toils and the sacrifices of forty years are crowned so successfully and hap-

pily, now that the great building is at last finished and ready to be used for divine purposes, need we say that we draw near an event whose consummation is to us as a people momentous in the highest degree? Far-reaching in its consequence, as that occasion is certain to be, what remains for us to say in order to impress the entire Church with a sense of its tremendous importance?

The letter continues with much counsel to the Latter-day Saints to repent of all sins, to divest themselves of every harsh and unkind feeling against each other; to replace such feelings with feelings of charity and love for one another; to yield obedience unto the commandments of God. The letter then reads:

> Thus may we come up into the holy place with our hearts free from guile and our souls prepared for the edification that is promised! Thus shall our supplications, undisturbed by a thought of discord, unitedly mount into the ears of Jehovah and draw down the choice blessings of the God of Heaven![39]

Many interesting spiritual experiences marked the dedication services, witnessing the acceptance of his house by the Lord. President Wilford Woodruff, who offered the dedicatory prayer, revealed to the assembled Saints that the hosts in the spirit world had joined in the dedication. He solemnly testified:

> I feel at liberty to reveal to this assembly this morning what has been revealed to me since we were here yesterday morning. If the veil could be taken from our eyes and we could see the spirit world, we would see that Joseph Smith, Brigham Young and John Taylor had gathered together every spirit that ever dwelt in the flesh in this Church since its organization. We would also see the faithful apostles and elders of the Nephites who dwelt in the flesh in the days of Jesus Christ. In that assembly we would also see Isaiah and every prophet and apostle that ever prophesied of the great work of God. In the midst of these spirits we would see the Son of God, the Savior, who presides and guides and controls the preparing of the kingdom of God on earth and in heaven.
> From that body of spirits, when we shout "Hosannah to God and the Lamb!" there is a mighty shout that goes up of "Glory to God, in the Highest!" that the God of Israel has

permitted his people to finish this Temple and prepared it for the great work that lies before the Latter-day Saints.

These patriarchs and prophets, who have wished for this day, rejoice in the spirit world that the day has come when the saints of the Most High God have had power to carry out this great mission.

There is a mighty work before this people. The eyes of the dead are upon us. The dedication is acceptable in the eyes of the Lord. The spirits on the other side rejoice far more than we do, because they know more of what lies before in the great work of God in this last dispensation than we do.

The Son of God stands in the midst of that body of celestial spirits, and teaches them their duties concerning the day in which we live and the dedication of this temple. . . .[40]

Today, as I reflect upon the pleasant years I have spent in the Salt Lake Temple, an interesting experience comes to memory. I was in the solemn assembly room. It was here that the Saints had met to dedicate the temple. I was listening to President Harold B. Lee answer questions of missionaries who were then in the missionary home in Salt Lake City, receiving instruction and training prior to their departure for their world-wide missions. Each Monday morning about three hundred of these missionaries were privileged to meet in the assembly room to be instructed by the prophet.

On this particular morning one of the missionaries asked the question, "President Lee, does the Savior ever visit the Salt Lake Temple?" It was a very unusual question to be asked and everyone seemed to lean forward in the seat to hear the answer.

After a moment's reflection, the prophet replied, "Son, how do you know he is not here now? *This is his house.*"

Like all the temples built and dedicated to his name in this dispensation, the Salt Lake Temple is *his house*. It is, in its construction, one of the wonders of the world. It is truly *poetry in stone* and is a structure worthy of the name it bears—*"The House of the Lord."*

Within its majestic walls the sacred rites and ordinances of baptism, ordination to the holy priesthood, bestowal of the holy endowment, celestial marriage, and the sealing of wife to husband and children to parents in an eternal family relationship are being administered.

And this glorious work is destined to continue, even into the millennium, in the temples of God that now exist and the incomparably greater number that shall yet be built under the command and direction of God, until the holy endowments and ordinances required for the eternal life of man shall have been extended to every soul, living and dead, who, in the knowledge and wisdom of God, is worthy to receive these sacred blessings.

NOTES

1. Exodus 33:7-8.
2. Exodus 33:11.
3. Exodus 25:2, 8-9.
4. Exodus 39:42-43.
5. Moroni 7:8.
6. Exodus 40:34,38.
7. 1 Samuel 1:9,24.
8. 1 Chronicles 14:1.
9. 1 Chronicles 17:1.
10. William Smith, ed., *Dr. William Smith's Old Testament History* (New York: Harper and Brothers, 1891), p. 232.
11. 1 Chronicles 17:2-5.
12. 2 Chronicles 2:3-9.
13. Smith, *Old Testament History*, p. 482; see also 2 Chronicles 2:13; 4:16.
14. Smith, *Old Testament History*, p. 483.
15. 1 Kings 8:1,6,10-11.
16. Matthew 21:13.
17. Matthew 27:51.
18. Smith, *Old Testament History*, pp. 227-228.
19. James E. Talmage, *The House of the Lord*, 1976 ed. rev. (Salt Lake City: Bookcraft, Inc., 1962), p. 52.
20. Moses 5:5.
21. Moses 5:6-7.
22. Christian Frederick Cruse, *The Ecclesiastical History of Eusebius Pamphili*, pp. 26-27. *The History of the Church from Christ to Constantine*, ed. G.A. Williamson (New York: New York University Press, 1966), pp. 46-47.
23. Moses 6:58-68.
24. Flavius Josephus, *Josephus Complete Works*, "Antiquities of the Jews," bk. 13, ch. 3, nos. 1-2, ed. William Whiston (Grand Rapids, Michigan: Kregel Publications, 1960), p. 269.
25. Josephus, *Complete Works*, "Antiquities of the Jews," bk. 13, ch. 3, no. 3, p. 269.
26. 2 Nephi 5:16.
27. D&C 36:8.
28. D&C 95:13-14.
29. *History of The Church of Jesus Christ of Latter-day Saints*, 7 vols. (Salt Lake City: Deseret News, 1966), 2:434-35.
30. D&C 110:1-7, 9-10.
31. B. H. Roberts, *A Comprehensive History of The Church of Jesus Christ of Latter-day Saints*, 6 vols. (Provo, Utah: Brigham Young University Press, 1965), 3:279.
32. Roberts, *A Comprehensive History*, 3:280; *Woodruff's Journal*, entry for July 28, 1847.
33. Susa Young Gates and Leah D. Widtsoe, *The Life Story of Brigham Young* (New York: The MacMillan Company, 1931), pp. 104-105.

34. Gates, *The Life Story of Brigham Young,* p. 105.
35. *Journal of Discourses,* 26 vols. (London: Latter-day Saints' Book Depot, 1855-1886), 1:132-33.
36. *Journal of Discourses,* 21:299-300.
37. Talmage, *The House of the Lord,* p. 142.
38. *Journal of Discourses,* 1:14.
39. Talmage, *The House of the Lord,* pp. 129-30.
40. Archibald F. Bennett, *Saviors on Mount Zion* (Salt Lake City: Deseret Sunday School Union Board, 1950), pp. 142-43; from a stenographic report of the dedication of the Salt Lake Temple, 6 April 1893.

2

GLORIOUS PURPOSE
OF THE FATHER

It is idle thinking to suppose that we can comprehend the purpose of temples and the ordinances performed there unless we first understand our relationship to God, the Father, and his objectives with respect to his children.

By divine revelation, we have learned that we lived as intelligent, thinking, choosing, acting spirit beings before the world was[1]; and that our spirit beings are literally children of the living God and brothers and sisters of Jesus Christ, who was the Firstborn in the spirit[2] and the Only Begotten in the flesh.[3]

In the Master's vocabulary, the name *Father* displaces almost every other name for God. He taught us to address God in our prayers as "Our Father who art in heaven"[4]; and among his first words after his glorious resurrection were those contained in his charge to Mary Magdalene: ". . . go to my brethren, and say unto them, I ascend unto my Father, and your Father; and to my God, and your God."[5]

The Apostle Paul had the same lofty conception of man as a spirit child of God, as evidenced by his exhortation to his Hebrew brethren. In an effort to impress upon them the logic and importance of conforming their lives to the will of God, as embodied in the new religion they had embraced, Paul persuasively says:

> . . . we have had fathers of our flesh which corrected us, and we gave them reverence: shall we not much rather be in subjection unto the Father of spirits, and live?[6]

It was in no abstract, nor mere philosophical, sense that the Apostle conceived of God as the father of the spirits of men. Witness these words from his eloquent address to the men of Athens, as he stood in the midst of Mar's hill:

> Ye men of Athens, I perceive that in all things ye are too superstitious. For as I passed by, and beheld your devotions, I found an altar with this inscription, TO THE UNKNOWN GOD. Whom therefore ye ignorantly worship, him declare I unto you.
>
> God that made the world and all things therein, seeing that he is Lord of heaven and earth, dwelleth not in temples made with hands; neither is worshipped with men's hands, as though he needed any thing, seeing he giveth to all life, and breath, and all things; . . . as certain also of your own poets have said, For we are also his offspring.
>
> Forasmuch then as we are the offspring of God, we ought not to think that the Godhead is like unto gold, or silver, or stone, graven by art and man's device.[7]

The few verses I have taken from the scriptures constitute a very small part of the great body of holy writ attesting to the glorious truth that the spirit of man is of heavenly and divine lineage, fashioned in the very image of God's person, heir to all that such lineage and heredity imply and promise, even the boundless possibilities of becoming like unto his Heavenly Father.

In accordance with the divine plan of our Father to afford his spirit children the opportunity to become like unto him, the earth was created and the sons and daughters of God were sent here to obtain bodies of flesh and bone and the experiences and blessings of mortal life as a preparation for life eternal.

Unto Moses, whom God repeatedly called "my son,"[8] there was given a vision of this world and all its inhabitants, and then God declared, "And worlds without number have I created; and I also created them for mine own purpose; . . . For behold, this is my work and my glory—to bring to pass the immortality and eternal life of man."[9]

Immortality is a blessing which no man shall be denied.

An immortal spirit is man's heritage as a child of God; an immortal body is man's blessing as a result of his obedience to God's commandments in his premortal life. Because he kept his "first estate," he was rightfully "added upon" by receiving a mortal tabernacle at birth.[10] Through the transgression of Adam, death came into the world and man was temporarily deprived of his body of flesh and bone. Through the mercy and justice of God and in consequence of the atonement of Jesus Christ, the body will be restored to man in the resurrection, as an immortal body. The immortal spirit will take up its habitation in the immortal body, never again to be separated, and thus will be accomplished the immortality of man, and this without regard to whether he has been good, bad, or indifferent in mortal life, and regardless of whether or not he received the gospel or any of its ordinances.[11]

Eternal life, however, while embodying immortality, reaches far beyond this universal blessing. To have eternal life is to have a life like unto that of our Eternal Father, to become like unto and one with him, sharing all that is his to give; being heirs of God and joint heirs with Christ, creating earths and peopling worlds. Unlike immortality, which comes to all, eternal life comes as a result of keeping God's commandments fully, until we, in our eternal progression, become perfect, even as our Father in heaven is perfect.[12]

This is the challenge and summation of the Sermon on the Mount. To attain this perfection, this eternal life, man must accept the gospel of Jesus Christ in its fulness, comply with all its laws, submit himself to the will of God, and receive all required ordinances, which include (1) baptism of the water and the Spirit, (2) ordination to the Holy Melchizedek Priesthood, (3) the Holy Temple Endowment ordinances, (4) the ordinance of marriage in the new and everlasting covenant, and (5) the sealing of children to parents, thus creating eternal families, all of which ordinances will be more specifically treated later in this book. While the living receive the first two of these ordinances—baptism and bestowal of the holy priesthood—prior to entering the temple for the endowment and marriage, all ordinances for and in behalf of the dead, by direction of God, are now performed only in the temples of God.

Truly the gate is strait and the way is narrow that leadeth unto life eternal and, as the Master declared, "Few there be that find it."[13]

NOTES

1. Abraham 3:22-23.
2. D&C 93:21.
3. John 1:14.
4. 3 Nephi 13:9; Matthew 6:9.
5. John 20:17.
6. Hebrews 12:9.
7. Acts 17:22-29.
8. Moses 1:4, 6-7.
9. Moses 1:8, 33, 39.
10. Abraham 3:26.
11. 1 Corinthians 15:20-22; Alma 11:43-44.
12. Matthew 5:48.
13. Matthew 7:14.

3

WHENCE THIS
STRANGE RITE

Early each morning, while most of the city sleeps, something which the world might consider very strange takes place. Groups of youth, boys and girls twelve years of age or a little older, enter the Salt Lake Temple and proceed quietly, reverently and anxiously to dressing rooms adjacent to a large room below ground level. The center of this large room is occupied by a spacious baptismal font, similar to the great "molten sea" in the Temple of Solomon,[1] resting on the backs of twelve life-sized, bronze-coated, cast iron oxen. The oxen are arranged in groups, three facing each cardinal point of the compass. The great font contains about four hundred gallons of water. It is below ground level, since baptism symbolizes a burial with Christ.

The youth, who have dressed in white clothing, descend, and each in turn is immersed in water by an authorized servant of God, for and in behalf of deceased persons whose names appear on a teleprompter in view of the living proxy, the officiator, the recorder, and two witnesses. The officiator raises his right arm to the square and, calling the youth by name, repeats the following revealed words: "Having been commissioned of Jesus Christ, I baptize you for and in behalf of (name of deceased) who is dead, in the name of the Father and of the Son and of the Holy

Ghost, Amen"; and then he immerses the living youth proxy in the water.

Whence came this strange ceremony, now practiced by Latter-day Saints alone in all the world?

Many years ago, while I served as president of the Chicago Stake, a young boy of deacon age from Milwaukee, Wisconsin, came to me with a temple recommend signed by his bishop and to be signed by me, which would authorize his being baptized for the dead in the Salt Lake Temple. I took the recommend into my hand, but before signing it or interviewing him as to his worthiness to enter the temple, I decided to find out what he knew about that strange rite of baptism for the dead.

I asked, "Why do you want to go to the temple?"

He quickly replied, "To be baptized for the dead."

Then, feigning surprise, I asked, "Why in the world do you want to be baptized for the dead?"

In a voice that expressed equal surprise, he responded: "I don't know; my dad got me into this."

Well, I explained the matter to him, interviewed him and gave him the recommend. As I subsequently relived this experience and thought of that amusing answer, "I don't know; my dad got me into this," I said to myself, "Well, that's as much as the world generally knows about the subject." I was carried back in memory to an experience I had as a teen-age missionary in western Massachusetts.

I was tracting in a suburb of Springfield. Several kind, Christian women who met me at their doors sympathized with such a poor boy who believed in the visions of Joseph Smith and counselled me to go to a certain minister in the community, assuring me that he would set me right in the matter of religion. I was not entirely unacquainted with this man. He was a prominent minister whose picture had often appeared in the newspapers in connection with lectures he had given in Springfield, Boston and other cities.

The challenge to visit him became irresistible, and before long I found myself at the entrance to his home. I had some fear in my heart that his superior knowledge of the Bible would prove embarrassing to me, but I knew the gospel was true and I had never knowingly passed up a minister's home while tracting; in fact, I had also made a friend or two among them. Mustering up my courage, I rang the door bell.

The door opened and a woman, whom I judged to be a domestic, faced me with that "what-do-you-want" look. I introduced myself as a Mormon missionary and said that I was a servant of the Lord and had come with a message for the man who lived there. While she was giving me the expected "brush-off," I heard a voice from the rear part of the house, "Let him come; let him in."

Ushered to the study, I found myself in the presence of the minister and his wife, both relaxed and reading. He wore no jacket, no collar, no vest on backwards, to indicate his profession. "Did I hear you say you had a message for me from the Lord?" he asked.

"Yes," I replied.

"Well, what is it?"

I gave him the message which, in essence, was that God had again opened the heavens and revealed himself to man; that he had raised up a prophet, Joseph Smith, and had restored the gospel which had been lost to the world; that he had reestablished his Church on the earth and had called missionaries to proclaim this message to the world.

"Do you then believe that the Mormon Church is the only true church in the world?"

"Yes," I replied, "that's what the Lord told Joseph Smith."

"Do you know that I am a Christian minister, myself?" he asked.

"Yes, that's why I came here," I responded. "I have met many of your congregation; they told me to come and see you and that you would straighten me out in my religious beliefs." A spontaneous laugh by both of us cleared the air and relieved the tension.

An interesting discussion ensued concerning what would happen to the rest of the world if the Mormons alone had the true religion. Explaining the plan of salvation for the dead, I took occasion to quote verse 29 from chapter 15 of Paul's first letter to the Corinthians, as it appears in the King James translation of the Bible:

> Else what shall they do which are baptized for the dead,
> if the dead rise not at all? Why are they then baptized for the
> dead?

"Young man, I think you are misquoting the scripture,"
he said.

"No, sir, that was a verbatim quotation," I replied.

He asked from which biblical version I had quoted. "The
King James version," I replied. Whereupon, he opened a
copy of the King James version. Finding the wording to be as
I had quoted, he expressed the opinion that it must be a
mistranslation which would not appear in a better version of
the Bible.

His wife, who had been listening to our friendly conversation, stepped to a bookcase, removed a book, and handed
it to her husband. Glancing at the book, he said that it was
one of the better versions of the Bible. He opened it and read
aloud these words:

> Else what shall they do who are baptized in behalf of the
> dead, if the dead rise not at all? why are they then baptized in
> behalf of the dead?

I could not resist saying, "I believe that is a better translation."

Had the minister answered the question, "Why baptism
for the dead?" with the same candor as the Milwaukee boy,
he might well have replied, "I don't know; Paul got us into
this."

This scriptural passage, inserted by Paul in his letter to
the Corinthians, is the sole, direct biblical reference to baptism for the dead. It has caused no end of discussion and
debate on the part of biblical scholars and polemic divines.
Certain of the Greek fathers have rendered it, Else what shall
they do who are baptized "in expectation of the resurrection
of the dead."[2] But this translation forces the grammar and
fails to make good sense. Kirsopp Lake, professor of New
Testament exegesis and the history of early Christian literature at the University of Leyden, has written, "It is impos-
sible that 'Else what shall they do who are baptized for the
dead? If the dead are not raised at all, why then are they

baptized for them?' can refer to anything except vicarious baptism."[3]

Granted that the text is authentic, there are many who brand the principle and rite of baptism for the dead as false, heretical and apostate. I ask: "Would Paul make use of a false doctrine to establish the truth of the resurrection in the minds and hearts of the Corinthians? Would he resort to a heretical doctrine and practice to prove the reality of the central doctrine of Christianity? Or was he unlearned in the matter of Christian doctrine?"

Paul was unquestionably the most learned among the Apostles in the primitive Church and was one of the greatest biblical scholars and writers of all time. In view of the text itself and the purpose for which Paul advances it, is it not logical to assume that the doctrine and rite of baptism in behalf of the dead was generally known, understood and practiced in the early Christian Church, and, furthermore, that Paul placed the stamp of approval upon it?

Whence came this vicarious baptismal rite? In volume I of the *Dictionary of the Apostolic Church*, we read: "There is no evidence that it [baptism for the dead] existed in the 1st cent., and the practice may have originated from this verse [1 Corinthians 15:29]."[4]

Surely it cannot reasonably be contended that even though Paul alone refers to it specifically that he is, therefore, the author of the doctrine and rite—the source from whence it sprang. Paul takes no credit for any of the Christian principles or practices. He bore witness to the Galatian Saints:

> . . . I certify you, brethren, that the gospel which was preached of me is not after man.
> For I neither received it of man, neither was I taught it, but by the revelation of Jesus Christ.[5]

It is highly untenable for the Christian world to accept Paul's epistle to the Corinthians as divinely inspired and, for want of understanding, to reject part of it as heresy. But such was the case, and in the year A.D. 393 the sixth Canon of the Synod of Hippo forbade the practice of baptism for the dead.

It seems to be historically true that man has found it most difficult, particularly in the field of religion, to admit that ideas which are beyond his comprehension may nevertheless conceivably be true. A good illustration of this is found in the *Dictionary of the Apostolic Church,* from which I have already quoted. This dictionary was edited by James Hastings, D.D., assisted by John A. Selbie, D.D., and John C. Lambert, D.D. The author writes:

> Whatever view is taken of *baptism for the dead* (1 Cor. 15:29) it alludes to the Christian rite. . . . Could St. Paul have even tacitly approved of such a thing? . . . It is probable that the problem is insoluble with our present knowledge, and that the reference is to some ceremony in the then baptismal rite at Corinth of which we hear no more, but not to vicarious baptism.[6]

It seems inconsistent that the author, after admitting that, with his present knowledge, the Christian rite of baptism for the dead was an insoluble problem, could not let the matter rest there without tacking on the illogical conclusion that baptism for the dead did not refer to "vicarious baptism." The text would be clear enough but for the attempts of "scholars" to explain it.

Without direct mention of baptism for the dead, Paul told the Hebrew Saints that they had a God-provided obligation to render a vicarious service in behalf of the dead. Having extolled the faith and virtues of many who lived prior to the coming of Christ in the flesh, he said:

> And these all, having obtained a good report through faith, received not the promise:
> God having provided some better thing for us, that they without us should not be made perfect.[7]

If the righteous dead cannot be made perfect without some necessary service to be performed in their behalf by the living, what is this vital service but the vicarious performance of the very same ordinances for the dead which are available to and required of the living?

The ordinances revealed by God and required for the salvation and exaltation of his children are timeless, dateless, eternal ordinances, applying with equal force and validity to all worlds, all nations, kindreds, tongues, and people—*living and dead*. The first ordinance is baptism (of the water and of the Spirit) "for the remission of sins,"[8] for entrance into the kingdom of God[9] and "to fulfil all righteousness."[10]

The first act of Jesus as he began his ministry at the age of thirty years was to present himself for baptism at the hands of John the Baptist. John, recognizing Jesus as the Christ, the very Son of God, protested, saying, "I have need to be baptized of thee, and comest thou to me?" Jesus answered him, "Suffer it to be so now: for thus it becometh us to fulfil all righteousness."[11]

Following his baptism, the first recorded statement of doctrine (sometimes called the first sermon) made by Christ was made in his conversation with Nicodemus, a ruler of the Jews, who sought out Jesus by night to learn what a man must do to enter the kingdom of God. Jesus proclaimed the basic law of baptism, saying, "Except a man be born of water and of the Spirit, he cannot enter into the kingdom of God."[12]

And the last message of the risen Christ to his apostles before his ascension into heaven, as recorded by Matthew and Mark, involved this important ordinance. Mark records Christ's charge to his chosen eleven as follows:

> And he said unto them, Go ye into all the world, and preach the gospel unto every creature.
> He that believeth and is baptized shall be saved; but he that believeth not shall be damned.[13]

Now, let me ask a few pertinent questions: If a man cannot enter into the kingdom of God without baptism, if a man cannot be saved except he "believeth and is baptized," if a man, though he were the Son of God, cannot fulfil all righteousness (by keeping all the commandments of God) unless and until he submits to the ordinance of baptism—in such case what shall be the fate of the millions who have died without having had the opportunity of learning of baptism or receiving its administration? Will a just God punish a man for not obeying a spiritual law of which he had no knowledge nor opportunity to receive knowledge? Does death before baptism remove the baptismal requirement? Could Jesus, understanding as he did the law of baptism, have fulfilled all righteousness by going to the grave without submission to it? Are there two plans of salvation—two gospels—one for the living and another for the dead?

Scripturally, there is but one plan for the salvation of mankind—"One Lord, one faith [gospel], one baptism"[14] and one name given under heaven whereby we must be saved, and that, as Peter declared, is "the name of Jesus Christ of Nazareth."[15]

Even if the laws of God pertaining to man's salvation could be waived by God, to waive them would not be an act of mercy on his part. He has revealed that

> There is a law, irrevocably decreed in heaven before the foundations of this world, upon which all blessings are predicated—
>
> And when we obtain any blessing from God, it is by obedience to that law upon which it is predicated.[16]

Thus, for God to waive the law would be to deprive man of the blessing he might otherwise have obtained by obedience to the law.

Our Father's plan for the salvation of man is and must be a perfect and universal plan, available to all men and not cut off at death, which comes to many almost simultaneously with birth. The Psalmist asks an age-old question:

> When I consider thy heavens, the work of thy fingers, the moon and the stars, which thou hast ordained;
>
> What is man, that thou art mindful of him? and the son of man, that thou visitest him?[17]

The simple answer is that man is the son of God, as Jesus clearly taught. What will God withhold from one son and give to another? Jesus asked:

> What man is there of you, whom if his son ask bread, will he give him a stone?
>
> Or if he ask fish, will he give him a serpent?
>
> If ye then, being evil, know how to give good gifts unto

your children, how much more shall your Father which is in heaven give good things to them that ask him?[18]

Through the ages, from the time of the loss of the gospel through apostasy in the early centuries after the death of Christ to its restoration in the nineteenth century, what did the so-called "Christian" religion offer to the non-Christian but an incomprehensibly unjust plan which would bar him forever from salvation, irrespective of the quality of his life, if he failed to believe in a Savior of whom he may never have heard or had the opportunity of accepting?

In the third article of its declaration of faith, The Church of Jesus Christ of Latter-day Saints asserts with conviction: "We believe that through the Atonement of Christ, all mankind may be saved, by obedience to the laws and ordinances of the Gospel." Thus, we proclaim to the world the hope and possibility of a universal salvation—a salvation to include all mankind.

Such a concept may run counter to the traditions and thoughts of the Christian world, but what other concept is worthy of an all-wise, loving God? Would the loving Father of all men devise a plan of salvation whose benefits were available to only a chosen few among all his children, to only those who heard and accepted the plan during mortal life? To what fate would he consign all others? Was Christ to be the Savior of all mankind or the Savior of only a small minority called Christians?

Let the thoughtful reader ponder the following questions: What provision has Christianity made for the salvation of the world? What has it to offer the non-Christian? It would appear that its offer must be limited to one of three alternatives.

First: That all men who have not accepted Christ, including those vast numbers who have never heard of him, are irretrievably and forever lost. Justice, mercy, and the love of God—the Father of all—cry out in opposition to such an abhorrent concept. Such a doctrine has no defense and needs no refutation.

Second: That the acceptance of Christ and his teachings is not required for salvation. This alternative, merciful though it appears, is contrary to the plain, unquestionable teachings of the Lord and his chosen servants, as has been pointed out.

Third: If neither of the first two alternatives is acceptable, then we are left with the inescapable remaining alternative which is that God, in his wisdom and justice, has provided a plan whereby all mankind, either during mortal life or after death, may learn of Christ, may accept him as the Christ, may be taught his gospel, and may have its saving ordinances made available to them. To the reality of this alternative the Latter-day Saints alone bear witness.

On the cross next to that on which Christ gave his life for all mankind, a repentant thief pleaded, "Lord, remember me when thou comest into thy kingdom."[19] To this plea Jesus responded with the promise, "Verily I say unto thee, To day shalt thou be with me in paradise."[20]

The Christian world generally has misinterpreted this promise as implying that the malefactor's deathbed repentance had won for him a place in heaven without compliance with the laws and ordinances of the gospel. However, the error in this conclusion is revealed by the admonition of the risen Lord to Mary Magdalene on the morning of his resurrection, three days after the promise was made.

When Mary, recognizing the living Christ, in joy cried out, "Rabboni"[21] and was about to embrace him, "Jesus saith unto her, Touch me not; for I am not yet ascended to my Father."[22] If Christ, on the third day after his crucifixion, had not yet ascended to his Father in heaven, where were he and the repentant malefactor on the day of his death and to what did he devote his attention during the interval between death and the resurrection? Christ's chief Apostle answers these questions in unmistakable language in his first general epistle. These are his words:

> For Christ also hath once suffered for sins, the just for the unjust, that he might bring us to God, being put to death in the flesh, but quickened by the Spirit:
> By which also he went and preached unto the spirits in prison;
> Which sometime were disobedient, when once the long-suffering of God waited in the days of Noah. . . .[23]

Thus, while Christ's body lay lifeless in the tomb, his living, intelligent, active spirit went to paradise to perform his divine service among the dead. The paradise referred to was not heaven but the abode of the spirits of the righteous and the repentant. The thief was not given immediate salvation and a place in the kingdom of heaven as a reward for his incipient repentance but was granted the privilege of hearing the gospel of Jesus Christ, God's plan of salvation. Explaining the purpose of teaching the gospel to the dead, Peter declared:

> For for this cause was the gospel preached also to them that are dead, that they might be judged according to men in the flesh, but live according to God in the spirit.[24]

This mission of Christ to preach to those of the dead who were imprisoned was foretold by Isaiah and was also proclaimed by Jesus himself, who bore witness to the reality of his approaching mission among the dead in this significant declaration to the Jews: "Verily, verily, I say unto you, The hour is coming, and now is, when the dead shall hear the voice of the Son of God: and they that hear shall live."[25]

It is readily understandable that the immortal, thinking, acting spirit of man, when separated from the physical body by death, could learn of Christ and be willing to accept and yield obedience to his teachings. If the dead could not hear and learn and believe, why preach to them? God, in his mercy, his justice, and his infinite wisdom, has provided the way for all his children to learn the gospel, believe, and receive the required ordinances, beginning with baptism, that are necessary for them to have a place in the Father's kingdom where Christ and God dwell.

The dead, themselves, must be highly concerned with the work that is being done for them in the temples of the Lord. Brigham Young is quoted as saying:

> What do you suppose the fathers would say if they could speak from the dead? . . . Why, if they had the power the very thunders of heaven would be in our ears, if we could but realize the importance of the work we are engaged in. . . .[26]

During the year 1877, being the year in which the St.

George Temple was dedicated and the work for the dead was commenced therein, Wilford Woodruff, then an Apostle and president of the temple, made an interesting entry in his journal:

> August 21, 1877. I, Wilford Woodruff, went to the Temple of the Lord this morning and was baptized for 100 persons who were dead including the signers of the Declaration of Independence except John Hancock and William Floyd. (John Hancock had already been baptized, 29 May 1877, and endowed, 30 May 1877, by Levi Ward Hancock, his 3rd cousin.)[27]

Subsequently, on a number of occasions, President Woodruff gave an interesting, detailed account of the circumstances which led him to perform this service. In the last general conference he ever addressed, he bore this sacred testimony:

> Another thing I am going to say here, because I have a right to say it. Every one of those men that signed the Declaration of Independence, with General Washington, called upon me, as an Apostle of the Lord Jesus Christ, in the Temple at St. George, two consecutive nights, and demanded at my hands that I should go forth and attend to the ordinances of the House of God for them. . . . I bear this testimony, because it is true.[28]

The ordinances which these dead needed and demanded were not limited to baptism only. Matthias F. Cowley records that in his advanced age

> Much of President Woodruff's meditations, as well as his hopes and ambitions, were associated with the world beyond the veil, and yet he was not in the least sense a fanatically visionary man. When he had important dreams they were in harmony with his religious conceptions and a part of his duty, both to man and God. On the night of March 19th, 1894, he had a dream which followed his meditations upon the future life and the work that he had done for the dead. In his dream there appeared to him Benjamin Franklin for whom he had performed important ceremonies in the House of God. This distinguished patriot, according to his dream, sought further blessings in the Temple of God at the hands of his benefactor. President Woodruff wrote: "I spent some time with him and we talked over our Temple ordinances which

had been administered for Franklin and others. He wanted more work done for him than had already been done. I promised him it should be done. I awoke and then made up my mind to receive further blessings for Benjamin Franklin and George Washington."[29]

To what extent the dead may have an awareness of and interest in what the living are doing may, generally, be a matter of conjecture and speculation. However, in view of the fact that, as Paul clearly states, those who die without having received the gospel ordinances cannot be made perfect without the aid of the living, it would appear an obvious conclusion that the righteous dead must be vitally concerned about receiving these ordinances vicariously. And, in view of President Woodruff's experience, who would question the possibility that certain of the worthy dead may be permitted by God to make their desires and needs known to mortals?

Though the plan of salvation for the dead is set out in the Bible, without modern revelation given in clarity to the Prophet Joseph Smith neither he nor we would have discovered it. We would still be viewing "through a glass, darkly"[30] our Father's just and beneficent plan with its rites and ordinances. We then might well say that "the problem is insoluble" and that with respect to baptism, "we don't know; Paul got us into this."

NOTES

1. 1 Kings 7:23-26.
2. *Dictionary of the Apostolic Church,* ed. James Hastings (New York: Charles Scribner's Sons, 1916), 1:128.
3. *Encyclopedia of Religion and Ethics,* ed. James Hastings et al. (New York: Charles Scribner's Sons, 1913), 2:382.
4. *Dictionary of the Apostolic Church,* 1:128.
5. Galatians 1:11-12.
6. *Dictionary of the Apostolic Church,* 1:128-29.
7. Hebrews 11:39-40.
8. Articles of Faith, 4; D&C 33:11.
9. John 3:5.
10. Matthew 3:15.
11. Matthew 3:14-15.
12. John 3:5.
13. Mark 16:15-16; see also Matthew 28:19-20.
14. Ephesians 4:4-5.
15. Acts 4:10-12.
16. D&C 130:20-21.
17. Psalm 8:3-4.
18. Matthew 7:9-11.
19. Luke 23:42.
20. Luke 23:43.
21. John 20:16.
22. John 20:17.
23. 1 Peter 3:18-20.
24. 1 Peter 4:6.
25. John 5:25.
26. *Journal of Discourses,* 18:304.
27. Wilford Woodruff, *Journal of Wilford Woodruff,* entry of August 21, 1877.
28. Wilford Woodruff, in Conference Reports, April 10, 1898, pp. 89-90.
29. *Wilford Woodruff, History of His Life and Labors,* comp. Matthias F. Cowley (Salt Lake City: Bookcraft, Inc., 1964), p. 586.
30. 1 Corinthians 13:12.

4

THE POWER TO GIVE
AND RECEIVE

It was the autumn of 1921. The Melchizedek Priesthood had been conferred upon me two years earlier, and I had been ordained an elder. I was now a Mormon missionary serving in the Eastern States Mission and was in charge of the work in the New Haven Conference—the Church name for an area covering the state of Connecticut and part of western Massachusetts.

There were extensive wooded areas, sparsely populated, outside the Connecticut cities. In those days, providing missionaries with automobiles, or even bicycles, for their work was not even a dream. If public transportation were not available, missionaries walked. Two elders asked for permission to travel through the woods some distance from New Haven and do missionary work without purse or scrip. Permission having been granted, they set out on a two-weeks venture.

At the end of the venture, the missionaries returned and made a report of the joys and successes and the trials and hardships they had encountered. They had not completely recovered from a very frightening experience. A man whose fact-sources had not been carefully selected had built up such a prejudice against the Mormons, none of whom he had ever met, that the mere mention of the name "Mormon" filled him with uncontrollable hatred. When the missionaries identified themselves at his home, he turned, picked up a shotgun, and levelling it at the missionaries' heads, gave them a certain number of seconds to be out of the gate and off his property or "I will fill you with lead," he warned.

One look at his face and the missionaries knew protests and conciliatory efforts would be vain. Faced with the obvious choice of running or dying, they chose to run. Clearing his property in half the allotted time, they did not stop until they were out of shotgun range. What an experience in a Christian community in the twentieth century!

One of the highlights of their trip was to be graciously invited to spend a night in a home where the family listened with great interest to the story of the gospel restoration. The family consisted of a father, a mother, and an adult, unmarried daughter who had a visible body deformity. It was a good Christian family. The mother was so well acquainted with the biblical record that the missionaries could scarcely refer to a scripture in their discussion that she could not quote verbatim.

This was a contact that should be maintained, and, a few weeks later, I called at this home in the backwoods of Connecticut. My reception by the family was heart-warming, and I spent an afternoon and evening explaining the gospel to them. I left the following morning with a pressing invitation to return for Thanksgiving dinner, at which all the children would be present as they were each Thanksgiving Day.

I could hardly wait for the day to come. It would be such a great missionary opportunity! The day came and found me riding the train to a stop in the woods, a short distance from the home. I was alone. The missionaries who had made the initial contact with the family had been transferred. We had an uneven number of missionaries in the conference, and I, of necessity, often travelled without a companion. The other New Haven elders were spending the day with the Saints in the city.

The roads and woods were blanketed in deep snow. I was met at the railroad stop and enjoyed a cold ride in a "one-horse open sleigh." I found the home warm and inviting and filled with the same gracious welcome I had experienced before. Mother and daughter were busily preparing the customary Thanksgiving dinner. The table was set for all the expected children and there was a feeling of excitement and anticipation in the home.

The hour for dinner arrived, but no children had come home. How unusual! "What could have happened?" mother and daughter were asking each other. There was no way of checking on the children since there was no telephone in the home. The minutes rolled on. We waited. An hour passed and yet another and still no children.

A thought occurred to me. "Did you tell your children that you had invited me to dinner?" I asked.

"Why, yes, I told them I had invited a Mormon elder to eat with us. Surely that would not keep them from coming home," she replied.

But it had, as I learned later. My presence was the cause of their absence. Finally, we sat at dinner. Only four of the many place settings were used. It was a sad little family and a doubly sad missionary, trying to make the best of a painful situation.

Dinner was over, the table was cleared, and the dishes put away. The evening shadows were falling. Suddenly another one-horse open sleigh pulled up in front of the home and a grave-faced man appeared in the doorway. In a tense voice, filled with emotion, he told his mother that his baby son was dying; that the doctor had been to their home, had examined the child, and had left telling them that the child would not live to see the morning.

The son had come for his mother. I soon learned that this good Christian woman had not merely an acquaintance with the scriptures but that she had a deep and abiding faith in them. Seemingly, without hesitation, she repeated the admonition of James, "Is any sick among you? let him call for the elders of the church; and let them pray over him, anointing him with oil in the name of the Lord: And the prayer of faith shall save the sick, and the Lord shall raise him up."[1] Then she continued, and I knew it was coming, "We have an elder right here in our home." Introducing me to her son, she asked if I would go with them and heal the child.

I was relieved when her son immediately protested that he hadn't come there for me; he had come for his mother. He made it clear that he had no desire for any prayer on my part. His mother pressed him, but he was adamant.

Embarrassed, I left the room. From an adjoining room I could hear bits of the conversation: the mother appealing to her son to have me bless the baby, the son replying that he wanted nothing from a Mormon elder. The mother was not to be denied. She came to the door and asked me if I would go with them and bless the baby. I explained that the blessing should not be forced upon her son and that I would go only if he asked me to do it. Another conversation between mother and son followed. Finally, reluctantly, he came to the door of the room where I was sitting and asked me to come with them and pray for his son.

Mother, son, and I were soon speeding across the snow in the open sleigh. Mother and son were anxiously talking about the baby who had not slept for many hours and who the doctor said would not survive the night. An anxious but quiet missionary sat in the seat beside them considering the challenge before him. I was embarrassed that this woman had more faith in the power of a Mormon elder than I myself had. I desperately wanted to heal the child. I silently prayed and prayed. I thought of the priesthood I held and of some of the promises God had made to those who exercised it in righteousness and in faith. There would be no question about the worthiness of a baby to receive the blessing, I reminded myself. It was a question of the will of God and of my faith.

I recalled the scripture: "And he ordained twelve, that they should be with him, and that he might send them forth to preach, and to have power to heal sicknesses, and to cast out devils."[2] I recalled many miracles performed by the disciples in the name of Jesus Christ and by the power of the priesthood he had conferred upon them. I particularly recalled the healing of the man "lame from his mother's womb," who begged alms at the gate of the temple, "which is called Beautiful"; of how Peter and John were asked for alms as they were about to enter the temple gate. And Peter fastened his eyes upon the man and said, "Look on us. . . ." Then Peter said, "Silver and gold have I none; but such as I have give I thee: In the name of Jesus Christ of Nazareth rise up and walk." And the beggar "leaping up stood, and walked, and entered with them into the temple, walking, and leaping, and praising God."[3]

I felt faith building up within me. I had no oil with which to anoint the child, but neither did the scripture tell of Peter using oil. I had no companion to assist me in the administration. Peter had John with him, but there was no record of John joining in the healing except possibly to share Peter's faith.

By the time we reached the home of the sick child, I was confident that God would hear my prayer. Taking the baby into my arms, I pronounced a blessing of life and health upon him by the power of the priesthood and in the name of Jesus Christ, and then I returned the baby to his mother who gently and tearfully laid her child in its crib.

Within minutes there was a sound of amazement and joy in the room. The child had taken on the appearance of health and well-being and was sleeping soundly and peacefully in the crib. A grateful mother thanked me; a grateful man drove his mother and me back to her home. Her faith was vindicated. A humble elder sat silent again. In his heart he was thanking God and pondering over the power of the priesthood which he could neither deny nor explain.

I left the next morning for New Haven, still marvelling over the experience of the previous night and wondering whether the apparent healing had been perfect and permanent. A few days later I received my answer. It came in a letter of gratitude from the child's father. His little son had slept peacefully through the night. The morning came, and he showed no sign of illness. The healing had truly been immediate, perfect and permanent.

Then, to my amazement, the letter went on to say that the father of the child was the same man who had threatened our missionaries with the shotgun and was ready to take their lives. He expressed sorrow and shame for his conduct; he hoped the missionaries would again come to his home and assured me that his home would always be our home.

As I contemplated the power of the priesthood in those days, I associated it with the healing of the sick, for this was its most obvious and demonstrable power. We do not see the priesthood; at best we but see its effects. The performance of baptism, the bestowal of the Holy Ghost, the giving of a patriarchal blessing, the temple ordinances, and all other gospel ordinances are administered by the power of the priesthood; but seldom do we observe any immediate, visible effect attesting to the validity of the ordinances.

There have been occasions when the bestowal of the gift of the Holy Ghost has been followed immediately by a spiritual manifestation, such as speaking in tongues as on the day of Pentecost.[4] Some similar manifestation must have occurred in the city of Samaria, where Philip preached with great success. He made and baptized many converts, but he could not bestow the Holy Ghost upon them since he did not possess the higher or Melchizedek Priesthood. Therefore, Peter and John went to Samaria and laid hands upon the newly baptized converts and conferred upon them the gift of the Holy Ghost.

One of the baptized converts—a rather questionable "convert"—was Simon, a sorcerer, who had a large following. As Peter and John performed the sacred ordinance, there must have come some miraculous manifestation of the efficacy of the ordinance which was witnessed by Simon. Envious as he was of this priesthood power exercised by Peter and John, you can almost hear Simon saying to himself, "If I could but add that power to my sorcery, what a profession I would then have; it would really pay off." So he approached Peter and John and "offered them money, Saying, Give me also this power, that on whomsoever I lay hands, he may receive the Holy Ghost."

Peter responded to this selfish attempt to obtain the priesthood power with the condemning words, "Thy money perish with thee, because thou hast thought that the gift of God may be purchased with money."[5]

As the years have passed, I have come to think of the

priesthood as a limitless power and authority, inherent in God and exercised by him for the eternal welfare of his children. God has revealed his beneficent purposes with respect to his children in these words, "Behold, this is my work and my glory—to bring to pass the immortality and eternal life of man."[6] For the accomplishment of this work the worlds are and were made and peopled.

Brigham Young defines priesthood in this colorful language:

> Priesthood . . . is the law by which the worlds are, were, and will continue for ever and ever. It is that system which brings worlds into existence and peoples them, gives them their revolutions—their days, weeks, months, years, their seasons and times and by which they are rolled up as a scroll . . . and go into a higher state of existence.[7]

I assume that the term *system* as used here by President Young is the equivalent of authority and power, for, to put it briefly, "Priesthood is the eternal authority and power of God."

This priesthood given of the Father to Christ in the premortal world enabled him, under the direction of the Father, to create our world and all things therein. This priesthood, delegated to Christ on earth, enabled him to create food for the multitudes in the desert,[8] to control the elements in stilling the waves and calming the Sea of Galilee,[9] to exercise power over life and death in the raising of Lazarus,[10] and finally to raise himself from the dead. He clearly taught that "As the Father hath life in himself; so hath he given to the Son to have life in himself."[11] And he further declared,

> Therefore doth my Father love me, because I lay down my life, that I might take it again.
> No man taketh it from me, but I lay it down of myself. I have *power* to lay it down, and I have *power* to take it again.[12]

This power of resurrection was a priesthood power given of God, the Father, to his Beloved Son. When man receives the priesthood, he receives it from God in whom it is inherent, and it is delegated to man to enable him to legally act for God in bringing to pass the eternal life of man. Joseph Smith clearly taught the Saints that "the Priesthood is an everlasting principle, and existed with God from eternity, and will to eternity, without beginning of days or end of years" and that "wherever the ordinances of the Gospel are administered, there is the Priesthood."[13]

I recall an interesting conversation with a minister in California while I presided over the California Mission a few years ago. Two of our missionaries had met him and interested him in the gospel. An appointment was arranged for him to come to my office in Los Angeles. After a brief discussion of certain gospel principles, our conversation focused on the restoration of the priesthood. The subject seemed to interest him greatly.

I had, under the glass top of my desk, a chart showing my priesthood lineage as a high priest, with pictures of the various individuals in the line of authority and, in most cases, dates of ordination. I had been ordained a high priest by one of the Lord's modern prophets, President Heber J. Grant, who was ordained an apostle by George Q. Cannon, who was ordained an apostle by Brigham Young, who was ordained an apostle by Oliver Cowdery, David Whitmer, and Martin Harris, Oliver Cowdery acting as spokesman, who, with Joseph Smith, had been ordained to the apostleship by Peter, James, and John, who were ordained apostles by the Lord, Jesus Christ.

I drew the minister's attention to this chart, and he stepped to the desk, examined it carefully, and expressed considerable interest in it. I asked him if he could trace his ministerial authority to Deity. He replied that he could not. He, of course, knew who had ordained him to the ministry, but that was the end of the line; he could go back no further and did not know how or where the man who ordained him had received the authority to do so.

He then frankly confessed that this matter had caused him much concern. He told me that while he had performed baptisms in the name of the Father, the Son, and the Holy Ghost, he had often asked himself whether and how he possessed the right to act in their names. His concern about this authority or lack of authority had recently reached the point where he had discontinued performing the baptismal ordinance personally and had turned this work over to the deacon of his church.

I repeat, any priesthood held by man is a delegated power and authority coming from God, in whom it is inherent. No man can take it upon himself.[14] Each man who possesses it must have received it, directly or indirectly, from God and can trace its source directly to Deity, from whom all priesthood is derived.

We are accustomed to think of priesthood as the authority and power to bestow blessings by the performance of gospel ordinances. However, of at least equal importance is the authority and power to *receive* which comes from the possession and right use of the priesthood.

Priesthood, like mercy in Shakespeare's words, "is twice blest;/It blesseth him that gives and him that takes."[15]

What may we receive through the possession and proper use of the priesthood? The answer is, we may receive all that the Father has to give, and this is included in the term *eternal life*.

To have eternal life is to have place in the highest glory of the celestial kingdom in the presence of the Father—to be able to endure the glory of his presence. To have eternal life is to attain to a life like unto the Eternal Father and to have like knowledge, purposes, powers, and character. The Prophet Joseph Smith equates eternal life with eternal lives, that is, to have the power of eternal increase. To have eternal life is to give birth and life to spirit offspring; to make provision for earthly tabernacles for these spirit children; to create and people worlds without number; to have power to bless and care for these children that they, in turn, may have the possibility of attaining eternal life with its joys and glories, powers and blessings. To have eternal life is to receive the gospel with all its priesthood ordinances, endowments, and blessings.

In short, to have eternal life is to receive all that the Father has to give; it is the Father's greatest gift.[16] No man, living or dead, receives it unless and until he has received the holy priesthood and has magnified his calling therein. Eternal life does not come easy nor in a sudden rush. It is the product of a life of obedience to the laws of God and of progress in righteousness that transcends mortal life and continues into eternity.

Now, specifically, just how and where does the holy priesthood have place in the attainment of eternal life? First and obviously, it bestows upon us the required gospel knowledge and ordinances. Beyond this, it provides us with power to receive all the blessings of God. If we would attain the knowledge of God and the mysteries of his kingdom that help us prepare for eternal life, then we must receive the holy priesthood. The Lord taught Joseph Smith this by a great revelation:

> And this greater priesthood administereth the gospel and holdeth the key of the mysteries of the kingdom, even the *key* of the *knowledge of God.*
> Therefore, in the ordinances thereof, the power of godliness is manifest.[17]

Do we desire to come into the presence of God, the Father, and be able to abide the glory of his presence, which is an important part of eternal life? If so, then we must receive the holy priesthood. Witness these words from the same revelation:

> And without the ordinances thereof, and the authority of the priesthood, the power of godliness is not manifest unto men in the flesh;
> For without this no man can see the face of God, even the Father, and live.[18]

Then the Lord continues this revelation by saying:

> Now this Moses plainly taught to the children of Israel in the wilderness, and sought diligently to sanctify his people that they might behold the face of God;
> But they hardened their hearts and could not endure his presence. . . .
> Therefore, he took Moses out of their midst, and the Holy Priesthood also.[19]

Referring to those who shall dwell in the presence of God, the Father, in celestial glory, the Lord said:

They are they who are priests and kings, who have received of his fulness, and of his glory:

And are priests of the Most High, after the order of Melchizedek, which was after the order of Enoch, which was after the order of the Only Begotten Son.[20]

Do we desire the blessing of eternal lives, of eternal offspring and all that this implies, including the power to create and people worlds? If so, we must enter into the sacred ordinance of eternal marriage. This is the significance of the instruction of the Prophet Joseph Smith, given at Ramus, Illinois, in May, 1843, under the inspiration of God. He said:

In the celestial glory there are three heavens or degrees;

And in order to obtain the highest, a man must enter into this order of the priesthood [meaning the new and everlasting covenant of marriage];

And if he does not, he cannot obtain it.

He may enter into the other, but that is the end of his kingdom; he cannot have an increase.[21]

Thus exaltation in the celestial glory, which is eternal life, is conditioned upon receiving and entering into the everlasting covenant of marriage. This everlasting covenant may now be entered into by the living, or by the dead through the proxy service of the living, *only* in the temples of God.

Entrance to the temple and the receiving of this sacred ordinance of marriage is available only to men who have received and honored the holy priesthood, and to their chosen companions who are sealed to them eternally in marriage, who become *one* with them, and who, while not possessing the priesthood, share in all the blessings of the priesthood which may come to the priesthood holder in time and in eternity.

In summary, let me draw attention to what the Lord has clearly declared, that no man may receive all the blessings that God, the Father, can bestow upon his children unless and until he has received the holy priesthood and has mag-

nified his calling within that priesthood. These are the words
of the Lord and his promise to the priesthood bearer:

> For whoso is faithful unto the obtaining these two priest-
> hoods of which I have spoken, and the magnifying their
> calling, are sanctified by the Spirit unto the renewing of their
> bodies.
>
> They become the sons of Moses and of Aaron and the
> seed of Abraham, and the church and kingdom, and the elect
> of God.
>
> And also all they who receive this priesthood receive me,
> saith the Lord;
>
> . . . And he that receiveth me receiveth my Father;
>
> And he that receiveth my Father receiveth my Father's
> kingdom; therefore all that my Father hath shall be given
> unto him.[22]

In the light of these revelations, how shall any man
receive "all that the Father hath" and become as God without the priesthood—the power and authority presently delegated to man from God and ultimately inherent in him, the
power to create and people worlds and to care for and bless
his eternal offspring?

Is it any wonder that great souls throughout the ages
have sought prayerfully and diligently for the priesthood
with its blessings? One of the greatest of the great was
Abraham, sometimes referred to as the "Father of the Faithful." He tells us: "I sought for mine appointment unto the
Priesthood according to the appointment of God unto the
fathers concerning the seed."[23] He further points out the
path he followed in obtaining the priesthood, with its rights
and powers, its happiness, peace, and rest. It was the path of
lofty desire, of righteousness, of willingness to receive the
counsel of God, and of dedication to keeping his commandments. Hear Abraham's words:

> In the land of the Chaldeans, at the residence of my
> father, I, Abraham, saw that it was needful for me to obtain
> another place of residence;
>
> And, finding there was greater happiness and peace and
> rest for me, I sought for the blessings of the fathers, and the
> right whereunto I should be ordained to administer the same;
> having been myself a follower of righteousness, desiring also
> to be one who possessed great knowledge, and to be a greater

follower of righteousness, and to possess a greater knowledge, and to be a father of many nations, a prince of peace, and desiring to receive instructions, and to keep the commandments of God, I *became a rightful heir, a high priest,* holding the right belonging to the fathers.[24]

I repeat, the priesthood is the authority and power delegated by God to man to bestow the ordinances and blessings of the gospel upon man. But the priesthood is not only the authority and power to *give,* it is also the power and authority to *receive.* When we contemplate even in part the blessings resulting from the possession and right use of the holy priesthood, we may grasp the significance of the words of the Lord to the elders returning in 1832 from their missions in the Eastern States:

> Wo unto all those who come not unto this priesthood which ye have received, which I now confirm upon you who are present this day, by mine own voice out of the heavens.[25]

NOTES

1. James 5:14-15.
2. Mark 3:14-15.
3. Acts 3:2-8.
4. Acts 2:1-4.
5. Acts 8:9-20.
6. Moses 1:39.
7. Brigham Young, *Discourses of Brigham Young*, sel. John A. Widtsoe (Salt Lake City: Deseret Book Co., 1941), p. 130.
8. Matthew 14:15-21; Mark 6:35-44; Luke 9:12-17; John 6:5-13; Matthew 15:32-38; Mark 8:2-9 (separate accounts of the miracles).
9. Matthew 8:24-27.
10. John 11:43-44.
11. John 5:26.
12. John 10:17-18; italics added.
13. Joseph Smith, *Teachings of the Prophet Joseph Smith*, sel. Joseph Fielding Smith (Salt Lake City: Deseret Book Co., 1938), pp. 157-8.
14. Hebrews 5:1,4-5,10.
15. Shakespeare, *The Merchant of Venice*, Act IV, scene 1.
16. D&C 14:7.
17. D&C 84:19-20.
18. D&C 84:21-22.
19. D&C 84:23-25.
20. D&C 76:56-57.
21. D&C 131:1-4.
22. D&C 84:33-38.
23. Abraham 1:4.
24. Abraham 1:1-2; italics added.
25. D&C 84:42.

5

THE HOLY
ENDOWMENT

From the beginning, because of our unusual and distinctive beliefs, practices, and way of life, Mormons have been thought of as a peculiar people. To the stranger in Salt Lake City, what could be more peculiar than to witness an unending procession of people, of all ages and at almost all hours of the day and night, filing in and out of the temple gates, carrying a bizarre assortment of luggage ranging from crocheted or knitted handbags to attaché cases and to suitcases of all shapes, sizes, and colors? What a curious sight to the stranger in the city! What brings all these people to the temple? And why the luggage?

Some of these people have come to perform baptisms for the dead; others to be married; still others to be sealed to parents. The majority, however, have come to receive what is known as the *endowment*. In their luggage the people bring clean, white clothing that they will wear while in the house of the Lord.

Just what is this "endowment" that hundreds of thousands of people come seeking? In the wisdom of God, the scriptures—ancient and modern—provide a meager source of information respecting the temple endowment. The Bible contains practically no information concerning the subject. As a matter of fact, I have found no biblical reference in which the term *endowment* is employed, and where the verb *endue* appears generally it is associated with such native endowments as talents, skill, power, ability, or with the blessing of family and posterity. The Doctrine and Covenants, which deals with most of our principles and practices in great detail, treats the endowment only in general and scanty terms.

The earliest reference to the *endowment* in this dispensation came from God in a revelation given through the Prophet Joseph Smith at Fayette, New York, on January 2, 1831, only nine months after the organizing of the Church. The Saints were commanded to go west and gather at the Ohio Valley. "There," said God, "I will give unto you my law; and there you shall be endowed with power from on high."[1]

The nature of the power was not revealed. During the next ten years, the Lord in his revelations to the Church repeatedly referred to an *endowment*. He commanded the Saints to build a house for him in Kirtland, told them it should be built after the manner and according to plans which he would reveal unto the Church, and directed them to appoint and ordain three brethren to receive the plans and dimensions from him, the Lord.

Hyrum Smith, Reynolds Cahoon, and Jared Carter were chosen and ordained for this purpose, and God revealed to them the plans for the sacred building. The purpose of this house was revealed in these words:

> Yea, verily I say unto you, I gave unto you a commandment that you should build a house, in the which house I design to endow those whom I have chosen with power from on high;
> For this is the promise of the Father unto you. . . .[2]

God revealed to the Prophet that it was expedient that the first elders of the Church receive an endowment in the house, that Zion could not be redeemed until the elders had received the "great endowment" and that the missionaries must receive this endowment before they were fully prepared to go unto all the world to teach the gospel and build up the Church.[3]

Thus the Lord had revealed the importance of the endowment without disclosing its nature. The Saints were left to anticipate, to hope for, and to await with eagerness the bestowal of the promised endowment.

How much the Prophet himself knew of the endowment at this time is not clear, but it undoubtedly exceeded what he had revealed to his associates. In a meeting with the Twelve at Kirtland, November 12, 1835, he made this interesting comment:

> The endowment you are so anxious about, you cannot comprehend now, nor could Gabriel explain it to the understanding of your dark minds. . . .
>
> But if we are faithful, and live by every word that proceeds forth from the mouth of God, I will venture to prophesy that we shall get a blessing that will be worth remembering, if we should live as long as John the Revelator; our blessings will be such as we have not realized before, nor received in this generation.[4]

The Kirtland Temple, built according to the plans and specifications which God had revealed to his chosen servants, was completed and was dedicated on March 27, 1836. The dedicatory prayer had been revealed by God to Joseph Smith, his prophet, and he dedicated this first house of the Lord in our dispensation.[5] In the early days following the dedication, the great endowment promised of God came upon the Church. During a sacrament meeting in the temple, exactly one week after its dedication, the Lord caused a pillar of light to rest upon his house, while angels came into it and a heavenly choir was heard joining with the Saints as they sang praises to their Lord and God.

After receiving the sacrament, the Prophet and Oliver Cowdery went behind the veil to pray. Here the Lord, Jesus Christ, appeared and spoke to them, telling them that he had "accepted this house" and that "the hearts of thousands and tens of thousands of people shall greatly rejoice in consequence of the blessings which shall be poured out, and the endowment with which my servants have been endowed in this house."[6]

Following Christ, there came a succession of the ancient

prophets who had stood at the head of former gospel dispensations, each conferring upon the Prophet Joseph and Oliver Cowdery the keys, powers and authority which they held under Christ. These prophets included Moses, who restored the keys of the gathering of Israel, and Elijah, who conferred the keys and sealing powers of the holy priesthood.[7]

What endowments these were! How would God fulfill his promises of old to gather scattered Israel and build up his earthly kingdom without providing his elders with the keys and powers to gather his people, Israel, from among the nations of the world? What would family life be, on earth or in heaven, without the keys and powers to seal wife to husband and children to parents and bind them into an eternally happy family?

In addition to these overall and world-blessing endowments, the Lord had prepared an individual and personal endowment to be given his Saints. The nature of this endowment was not recorded in detail in the scriptural record and would be known only to those who were worthy to receive it.

There has been some conjecture and even controversy as to the extent to which the endowment was known and received in Kirtland. It is true that certain of the initial ordinances of the endowment were received by many in the Kirtland Temple and that some of the brethren recorded in their journals and bore witness at general conferences of the Church that they had received the endowment in Kirtland. However, it would appear from subsequent revelations and events that the endowment, as we have it today, was not known nor revealed at Kirtland. This is evident from the revelation of the Lord commanding the Saints to build their next temple in Nauvoo. The language in this revelation precludes the possibility of the personal endowment having been revealed or practiced in its fulness in Kirtland. This is the interesting language used in the revelation:

> Verily I say unto you, let this house be built unto my name, that I may reveal mine ordinances therein unto my people;

For I deign to reveal unto my church things which have been kept hid from before the foundation of the world, things that pertain to the dispensation of the fulness of times.

And I will show unto my servant Joseph all things pertaining to this house, and the priesthood thereof. . . .[8]

The futurity of this language "I *deign to reveal* unto my church things which have been kept hid" and *"will show unto my servant Joseph all things pertaining to this house"* is rather clear evidence that the priesthood ordinances and blessings of the temple in their fulness had not been revealed nor given in Kirtland.

The revelation containing the commandment to build a temple at Nauvoo and the promise of the Lord to reveal all things pertaining to it to the Prophet had been given on January 19, 1841.[9] Some time between that date and May 4, 1842, God, pursuant to his promise, had revealed to his servant Joseph the endowment in its fulness and all other things pertaining to the temple.

Joseph did not wait for the erection of the Nauvoo Temple to share these great blessings with the Saints. How could he withhold the light and knowledge he had received until the temple was completed? His martyrdom was to occur two years before the completion of this temple. He records in his journal that he dedicated a room for sacred purposes above his brick store in Nauvoo.

In this room, he said, "I keep my sacred writings, translate ancient records, and receive revelations."[10] There, in that room, on May 4, 1842, he revealed and bestowed the holy endowment upon certain of his brethren. He writes:

> I spent the day in the upper part of the store . . . in council with General James Adams, of Springfield, Patriarch Hyrum Smith, Bishops Newel K. Whitney and George Miller, and President Brigham Young and Elders Heber C. Kimball and Willard Richards, instructing them in the principles and order of the Priesthood, attending to washings, anointings, endowments and the communication of keys pertaining to the Aaronic Priesthood, and so on to the highest order of the Melchizedek Priesthood, setting forth the order pertaining to the Ancient of Days, and all those plans and principles by which one is enabled to secure the fullness of those blessings which have been prepared for the Church of the First Born,

and come up and abide in the presence of the Eloheim in the eternal worlds.[11]

The Prophet goes on to say:

In this council was instituted the ancient order of things for *the first time* in these last days.[12]

Elder B. H. Roberts, one of the great scholars of this dispensation, wrote a footnote to the Prophet's journal entry in which he says:

This is the Prophet's account of the introduction of the Endowment ceremonies in this dispensation, and is the foundation of the sacred ritual of the temples.[13]

The following day the Prophet wrote in his journal:

General Adams started for Springfield, and the remainder of the council of yesterday continued their meeting at the same place, and myself and Brother Hyrum received in turn from the others, the same that I had communicated to them the day previous.[14]

It is interesting to consider some of the implications in the Prophet's language. He says that in giving the endowment, he was "setting forth the order pertaining to the Ancient of Days" and that he "instituted the ancient order of things for the first time *in the last days*." The *Ancient of Days* is a title belonging to one man, and one man only; that man is Father Adam. If, then, the "order" spoken of pertained to Adam, are we going too deep into the mysteries of the kingdom, or into the realm of speculation, to assume that the endowment was known to and probably received by the father of the human race? And if this blessing was given to Adam, would it not likely be conferred upon others through the years that followed?

But the history of the endowment and the extent to which it was known and administered prior to the present dispensation is not a matter of biblical reference. However, President Joseph Fielding Smith has expressed his conviction that Peter, James, and John received the endowment when they were with Moses, Elijah, and Christ on the Mount of Transfiguration.[15]

If we take into account the language of the Lord in the

revelation to Joseph Smith on January 19, 1841, to the effect that he would reveal unto his Church things that had been kept hidden from before the foundation of the world, things pertaining to this last dispensation, and show all things pertaining to the temple to his servant Joseph, we can come to but one conclusion, which is that the endowment and other temple blessings were not revealed or bestowed, *in their fulness*, in the former dispensations of the gospel.

I often wondered, as I read the Old and New Testaments in my earlier years, why God had withheld a fulness of light and truth from the world. The only answer I could come up with was that the world, because of unworthiness and lack of faith, was not prepared to receive such light and truth. Yet, even in recent years, I have searched the biblical record of the tabernacle built by Moses and the temples built in Jerusalem for some perceptible record of the holy endowment: but all in vain. And I closed the Bible saying to myself, "I guess if God intended to keep anything hidden from the world, he wouldn't publish it in the world's 'best seller.' "

The Nephite scriptures are even more silent with respect to temple teachings and practices. Nephi says of the first temple which his people built on this continent:

> And I, Nephi, did build a temple; and I did construct it after the manner of the temple of Solomon save it were not built of so many precious things; for they were not to be found upon the land, wherefore, it could not be built like unto Solomon's temple. But the manner of the construction was like unto the temple of Solomon; and the workmanship thereof was exceeding fine.[16]

This was followed by other temples, all without recorded explanation as to their purposes and use. Of one thing we are certain—there were no ordinances for the dead performed in any temple prior to Christ's crucifixion. The dead could not receive the gospel ordinances, directly or by proxy, before Christ's ministry among them during the three-day period following his death. As the prophets foretold, and as Peter reported, he opened the prison doors and preached the gospel of deliverance to those that were bound in chains of darkness.

I believe that the world has always been blessed with all the light and truth it was prepared to receive, that God withholds nothing from his children that they are worthy to receive and which would prove a blessing to them. To bestow sacred truths and ordinances upon an unprepared, unworthy, and faithless people would result only in their condemnation, and it is not the purpose of God to condemn the world.

For a time after the introduction of the endowment, it was bestowed upon others of the Saints in the upper room. Then it seems to have been discontinued pending the completion of the Nauvoo Temple. God had already stopped the performance of baptisms for the dead, which he had permitted the Saints to perform initially in the Mississippi River in the days of their poverty. The Prophet, in a doctrinal sermon delivered at a general conference at Nauvoo October 2, 1841, announced to the assembled Church:

> There shall be no more baptisms for the dead, until the ordinance can be attended to in the Lord's House; and the Church shall not hold another General Conference, until they can meet in said house. *For thus saith the Lord.* [17]

This was the stimulus the Saints needed to make the required sacrifices to build the temple. With gun in one hand to protect them from their enemies, and building tools in the other hand, dedicated workers "in the midst of trials, tribulations, poverty, and worldly obstacles, solemnized in some instances, by death,"[18] persisted in the construction of this second latter-day temple. Through their heaven-blessed labors, on October 5, 1845, the Saints met in the new house of the Lord in general conference.

The temple had been entirely closed in, the windows installed and temporary floors provided. Now it must be prepared for the bestowal of the endowment.

The enemies of the Church were pressing in on all sides. Brigham Young wrote in his journal: "There seems to be no disposition abroad but to massacre the whole body of this people, and nothing but the power of God can save us from the cruel ravages of the bloodthirsty mob."[19] Nevertheless the Saints continued their work on the temple.

Brigham Young recorded:

> Sunday, November 30, 1845. At ten a.m. I went to the
> attic story of the Temple [accompanied by twenty other
> Church leaders]. At about 12 o'clock, sang the song "Come
> All Ye Sons of Zion."
> I requested Wm. Clayton to keep minutes. I then offered
> up prayer and dedicated the attic story of the Temple and
> ourselves to God, and prayed that God would sustain and
> deliver us his servants from the hands of our enemies, until
> we have accomplished his will in this house.[20]

Then, it appears, the Saints concentrated their efforts on
the completion of the "east room." Brigham Young records
that on Wednesday, December 10, 1845, "at 3:45 P.M., we
completed the arrangements of the east room, preparatory to
giving endowments" and that at "four-twenty-five p.m.,
Elder Heber C. Kimball and I commenced administering the
ordinances of endowment . . . continued [through] the night
until three-thirty a.m. on the 11th."

They had administered these first endowments in the
Nauvoo Temple to fifteen brethren and fifteen sisters. After
Brigham and Heber had had breakfast at the home of Joseph
Kingsbury, they returned to the temple and, with other
members of the Twelve, administered the endowment to
fifteen more of the Saints—seven brethren and eight sisters,
including Lucy Mack Smith, mother of the Prophet Joseph
Smith.[21]

By December 26 two hundred and sixty-eight high
priests had received the endowment. The high priests
seemed to have been accorded some priority over other
brethren during the first few days after the endowments
were commenced, but President Young announced on the
twenty-sixth that they would pay no respect to quorums
thereafter. He called for a few days' rest for the Saints and
for the temple, during which he would select the persons to
officiate in the ordinances and would make regulations respecting the work. The rest lasted only through Sunday,
December 28, and then the work began again with increased
dedication.[22]

The endowment work continued with little interruption
until February 1846. A new motivation for the endowment

work may have come on January 2, 1846, as a result of a dream of Heber C. Kimball. Brigham Young records the dream in his journal:

> This morning Elder Heber C. Kimball related the following dream: Last evening, before retiring to bed he asked God to enlighten his mind with regard to the work of endowment; while sleeping he beheld a large field of corn that was fully ripe, he and a number of others were commanded to take baskets and pick off the corn with all possible speed, for there would soon be a storm that would hinder the gathering of the harvest. The hands engaged in gathering the harvest, were heedless and unconcerned and did not haste, as they were commanded; but he and the man he assisted had a much larger basket than the rest, and picked with all their might of the largest ears of the field, they once in a while would pick an ear that had a long tail on each end and but a few grains scattering over the center of the cob, which were very light.

Brigham Young then proceeds with the meaning of the dream:

> The interpretation of the dream is, that the field represented the church, the good corn represented good saints, the light corn represented the light and indifferent saints, the laborers are those appointed to officiate in the Temple, the storm is trouble that is near upon us, and requires an immediate united exertion of all engaged in giving the endowments to the saints, or else we will not get through before we will be obliged to flee for our lives.[23]

The endowment work continued with great intensity as the storm clouds gathered. Reports came pouring into Nauvoo from presumably reliable sources. It was reported that the Saints were about to be massacred if they did not leave Illinois immediately. Other reports were that they would not be permitted to leave, particularly as an armed body, lest they go to California and Oregon and, because of the great persecution they had suffered without protection from their own government, they should join an unfriendly nation and seek revenge.

On Sunday, January 11, the "General Council" of the Church met and arranged to make an early start west. The following day one hundred and forty-three persons received their endowments in the temple, and Brigham Young wrote:

Such has been the anxiety manifested by the saints to receive the ordinances [of the temple], and such the anxiety on our part to administer to them, that I have given myself up entirely to the work of the Lord in the Temple night and day, not taking more than four hours sleep, upon an average, per day, and going home but once a week.[24]

By Tuesday, February 3, the storm clouds were beginning to break and Brigham Young announced that no further endowment ordinances were to be administered in the temple. He writes:

Notwithstanding that I had announced that we would not attend to the administration of the ordinances, the House of the Lord was thronged all day, the anxiety being so great to receive, as if the brethren would have us stay here and continue the endowments until our way would be hedged up, and our enemies would intercept us. But I informed the brethren that this was not wise, and that we should build more Temples, and have further opportunities to receive the blessings of the Lord, as soon as the saints were prepared to receive them. In this Temple we have been abundantly rewarded, if we receive no more. I also informed the brethren that I was going to get my wagons started and be off. I walked some distance from the Temple supposing the crowd would disperse, but on returning I found the house filled to overflowing.

Looking upon the multitude and knowing their anxiety, as they were thirsting and hungering for the word, we continued at work diligently in the House of the Lord. Two hundred and ninety-five persons received ordinances.[25]

While some of the Saints were crossing the Mississippi with their wagons, others remained to receive their endowments in the face of death. Five hundred and twelve persons were endowed on Friday the sixth, and, "according to G.A. Smith's Journal, upwards of six hundred" were endowed on February 7.[26]

On Sunday, February 8, Brigham Young records:

I met with the Council of the Twelve in the southeast corner room of the attic of the Temple. We knelt around the altar, and dedicated the building to the Most High. We asked his blessing upon our intended move to the west; [we] also asked him to enable us some day to finish the Temple, and dedicate it to him, and we would leave it in his hands to do as he pleased; and to preserve the building as a monument to Joseph Smith. We asked the Lord to accept the labors of his servants in this land. We then left the Temple.[27]

This seems to have ended the giving of the endowments in the Nauvoo Temple, no less than 5,634 endowments having been administered there as reported in Brigham Young's journal. So far as the records reveal, all of those endowments were for the living; no endowments were performed in behalf of the dead prior to the dedication of the St. George Temple.

At 3:30 P.M. on February 9, the roof of the temple was discovered to be on fire. Brigham Young wrote:

> I saw the flames from a distance, but it was out of my power to get there in time to do any good towards putting out the fire, and I said if it is the will of the Lord that the Temple be burned, instead of being defiled by the Gentiles, Amen to it.[28]

So many of the Saints were forced to flee from Nauvoo without the blessing of the endowment that a new temple in the west became a favorite subject of discussion among the pioneers on their way to their new home. Four days after their arrival in the Salt Lake Valley, the site for the Salt Lake Temple was designated by Brigham Young acting under the inspiration of the Lord. However, in the days of their poverty, as in Nauvoo, the Lord provided for the Saints to receive the holy endowment in other chosen sanctuaries.

The first historically recorded endowment in the territory was administered on Ensign Hill (peak) on October 21, 1849.[29] During a general conference of the Church on October 6, "It was moved and seconded that Elder Addison Pratt, James Brown, and Hiram H. Blackwell, go to the Society Islands to preach the Gospel." The motion was carried and preparations were made for their departure. Addison Pratt had not received his endowment. Since it was the will of the Lord that the elders receive the endowment before going forth to preach the gospel and build up the kingdom, Elder Pratt was taken to Ensign Hill to be given the endowment. Brigham Young says of this incident: "Addison Pratt received his endowments on Ensign Hill on the 21st, the place being consecrated for the purpose."[30]

The first under-roof endowments in the Salt Lake Valley were given in the "Old Council House," which was the first permanent public building erected in Salt Lake City. It was a two-story, red sandstone building with a large hall and two office rooms on each floor. Standing on the southwest corner of the intersection of South Temple and Main Streets, the structure was commenced on February 26, 1849, and completed in December of 1850.

> It was designed as a "general council house" for the church; but was also used by the provisional "State of Deseret" as a "state house.". . . Under instructions from President Young, Heber C. Kimball on the 7th of July, 1852, resumed the administration of endowment ordinances to the saints in it, which privilege had been suspended since the expulsion from Nauvoo.[31]

On May 5, 1855, the Endowment House, built at the northwest corner of Temple Square, was dedicated and superseded the Old Council House as the endowment sanctuary.[32] "It . . . remained in use, with little interruption, for thirty-four years, when it was taken down by order of Wilford Woodruff, in the spring of 1889, because of rumors that plural marriages, contrary to the law of the land, were being solemnized in the building."[33]

On April 6, 1877, twelve years before the demolition of the Endowment House, the St. George Temple was dedicated. It should be noted that certain parts of the temple were dedicated on January 1, 1877, and immediately after that endowments began in this, the first temple completed in the territory of Utah. For the first time in this temple, on January 9, 1877, the ordinance of baptism for the dead was administered. Two days later, on January 11, Brigham Young announced in the temple during an endowment session "that this was the first time that the endowments had been administered for the dead (of which there was any record) in this dispensation."[34]

On April 8 Brigham Young appointed Wilford Woodruff to preside over the temple as its first president and charged him with the responsibility to "write all the ordinances of the Church from the first baptism and confirmation through every ordinance of the Church."[35] Brigham Young, Jr., was appointed to assist him in this writing project. Wilford Woodruff states that George Q. Cannon also "assisted some in this writing." It appears that as the writing progressed it was periodically presented to President Young for his approval.

When the writing of the endowment was finished to the satisfaction of Brigham Young, he said to Wilford Woodruff, "Now you have before you an ensample to carry on the endowments in all the temples until the coming of the Son of Man."[36]

I have dealt briefly with the history of the holy endowment and the early proclamations of God concerning its importance. But the question still remains "What is the *endowment?*" Because of its sacredness and the prohibitions of the Lord established to protect its sanctity, many of the beautiful ordinances of the holy endowment and much of the detailed instruction involved cannot be disclosed or presented except to those who are worthy to receive the ordinances and instruction in the place where God has decreed they shall be administered and revealed—in his holy house. However, there is still much that can be disclosed. In fact, much has been published regarding this subject.

During the spring of 1974 I accepted an invitation from the editor of the *New Era* to write a response to the question "What is a temple endowment?" for publication in the October issue of the magazine. In the course of preparation, I turned to the latest dictionary in my library and glanced at a few of the generally accepted definitions of *endow* and *endowment*, such as "to enrich," "to furnish with an income," "funds or other properties donated to educational and eleemosynary organizations and institutions." Suddenly my attention was drawn to a new, unusual, and unexpected definition relating to religion that read:

> A course of instruction in the Mormon Church concerning past and present dispensations and their associated ordinances and given in the temples only.[37]

I had hardly expected to find an attempt to define the Church endowment in a dictionary. I reread this definition and said to myself, "That is about as close to a definition of the temple endowment as one could come without knowing what it is." Good as it was, this definition fell far short of the eternal scope of the temple endowment.

The endowment is not limited to instruction pertaining to past and present dispensations and associated temple ordinances. The principles and ordinances of the endowment are timeless: they were ordained and established before the world was; they reach into eternity in two directions—forward and backward—and apply more importantly to futurity than to the past, while, at the same time, providing guidance, direction and strength to the present.

The endowment comprehends an enrichment not measured nor measurable in terms of money or other material treasures, which are subject to theft and the corrosion of moth and rust. To receive the endowment is to receive the riches of eternity—the knowledge, the power, the keys that unlock the door to the indescribable treasures of heaven and open the way to exaltation in the celestial world. To receive the endowment is to receive a course of instruction in eternal truth, together with all the keys, powers, and ordinances revealed and ordained of God to prepare his children for his greatest gift—the gift of eternal life.

The temple is an institution not only of higher learning but of the highest learning. In the temple, students are taught basic, changeless, everlasting truths applicable to time and eternity. Too often in the educational institutions of the world that which is advanced as truth is mere theory that might change before the student has graduated. This leaves us with some appreciation for Josh Billings's reported comment: "It ain't what a man don't know as makes him a fool; it's what he knows that ain't so."

I recall that some years ago a contest was sponsored by one of our national magazines involving the best definition of *truth*. The first prize was awarded a man in Michigan who submitted the definition: "Truth is that which temporarily has the appearance of permanence."[38]

One of the most intriguing questions asked of Jesus during his earthly ministry was asked by Pilate at the time of

Jesus' arraignment before him. Pilate inquired as to whether Jesus claimed to be a king. "Art thou a king then?" he asked.

"Jesus answered, Thou sayest that I am a king. To this end was I born, and for this cause came I into the world, that I should bear witness unto the truth. Every one that is of the truth heareth my voice."

Then Pilate asked the presumably unanswerable question that had been asked and discussed in vain by philosophers over the centuries: "What is truth?"

Jesus gave no recorded answer to the question. Apparently Pilate expected no answer, for the record states that as soon as he asked the question "he went out again unto the Jews."[39]

Nineteen hundred years later, Jesus gave a clear answer to the question in a revelation to the Prophet Joseph Smith: "Truth is knowledge of things *as they are, and as they were, and as they are to come.*"[40] Such are the truths contained in the endowment—knowledge of things, past, present, and future, *as they were, as they are,* and *as they are to come.*

The Prophet Joseph Smith's definition of the endowment is embodied in his journal entry of May 4, 1842, when he first revealed the endowment to his associates. He said he spent the day

> instructing them in the principles and order of the Priest-
> hood, attending to washings, anointings, endowments and
> the communication of keys pertaining to the Aaronic Priest-
> hood, and so on to the highest order of the Melchizedek
> Priesthood, setting forth the order pertaining to the Ancient
> of Days, and all those plans and principles by which any one
> is enabled to secure the fullness of those blessings which have
> been prepared for the Church of the First Born, and come up
> and abide in the presence of the Eloheim in the eternal
> worlds.[41]

Brigham Young, who received the endowment that day in the upper room, gives his definition of the endowment in more colorful language. In a talk he made on the southeast cornerstone of the Salt Lake Temple, after the First Presidency and the Patriarch had laid it, he said:

> Your *endowment* is, to receive all those ordinances in the

House of the Lord, which are necessary for you, after you have departed this life, to enable you to walk back to the presence of the Father, passing the angels who stand as sentinels, being enabled to give them the key words, the signs and tokens, pertaining to the Holy Priesthood, and gain your eternal exaltation in spite of earth and hell.[42]

In addition to the future blessings briefly stated by Joseph Smith and Brigham Young, there is in the endowment a source of present strength and guidance, which the Lord ordained that his missionaries should receive before going on their important errands. President Harold B. Lee adds this dimension to our understanding of the endowment in a definition given by him:

> The temple ceremonies are designed by a wise Heavenly Father who has revealed them to us in these last days as a *guide and protection throughout our lives* that you and I might not fail of an exaltation in the Celestial kingdom where God and Christ dwell.[43]

Because of the sacredness of the endowment and the obligations that those who receive the blessings of light and truth must necessarily take upon themselves, I say to our Latter-day Saint youth, "Do not rush to the temple to receive your endowment until you have the faith to keep the commandments of God and live in accordance with his will." It is my opinion that Church members should be authorized to obtain the endowment only when worthiness, age, and maturity justify it. Lacking worthiness and adequate preparation of mind and heart to receive the blessings of the endowment, it is better that we do not enter the house of the Lord where the light of truth burns so brightly, for light can condemn as well as bless. We should consider well the beautifully expressed concept of the endowment given us by James E. Talmage. He wrote:

> The ordinances of the endowment embody certain obligations on the part of the individual, such as covenant and promise to observe the law of strict virtue and chastity, to be charitable, benevolent, tolerant and pure; to devote both talent and material means to the spread of truth and the uplifting of the race; to maintain devotion to the cause of truth; and to seek in every way to contribute to the great preparation

that the earth may be made ready to receive her King—the Lord Jesus Christ. With the taking of each covenant and the assuming of each obligation a promised blessing is pronounced, contingent upon the faithful observance of the conditions. No jot, iota, or tittle of the temple rites is otherwise than uplifting and sanctifying.[44]

Unless we are prepared to take upon ourselves such obligations, we are not fully prepared to receive the endowment.

The temple may be thought of as the "Lord's University" where his eternal truths make up the curriculum. The courses of instruction begin with our premortal life and carry us on to celestial worlds, unfolding the plan of God for our salvation and exaltation in the eternal worlds until we become like unto him. The courses of instruction are not easy. God said, "I will show unto my servant Joseph all things pertaining to this house, and the priesthood thereof."[45] Only with his help would Joseph be able to comprehend the temple, its priesthood ordinances, and its blessings.

A full comprehension of the endowment, together with eternal marriage and family relationships, encompasses all our theology and transcends the limits of our finite minds. No matter how good and effective the pedagogy—the method and skill of teaching—I think we shall not, in this life, comprehend the endowment in its fulness. After years of service in the temple and much prayerful study and contemplation, my vision of the holy endowment has increased immeasurably. However, I know I have not mastered the subject.

What don't I know about it? I don't know, but I do know this: there are, in the endowment, truths that I have not yet comprehended, vistas of learning that I have not yet seen, and fields of wisdom and understanding which I have not yet even entered upon, much less explored and brought into possession. Considering the new light and understanding that continually comes to me as I serve in the house of the Lord, I feel that the endowment is a subject that I shall not exhaust in this life but that which I do know will ever be to me a "Pearl of Great Price."

NOTES

1. D&C 38:32.
2. D&C 95:8-9.
3. D&C 105:11-12,33.
4. *History of the Church,* 2:309.
5. D&C 109.
6. D&C 110:1-7,9.
7. D&C 110:11-16.
8. D&C 124:40-42.
9. D&C 124:25-28.
10. *History of the Church,* 5:1.
11. *History of the Church,* 5:1-2.
12. *History of the Church,* 5:2; italics added.
13. *History of the Church,* 5:2 (footnote).
14. *History of the Church,* 5:2-3.
15. Joseph Fielding Smith, *Doctrines of Salvation,* 3 vols. (Salt Lake City: Bookcraft, Inc., 1955), 2:165.
16. 2 Nephi 5:16.
17. *History of the Church,* 4:426.
18. *History of the Church,* 7:456.
19. Ibid., p. 481.
20. Ibid., p. 534.
21. Ibid., pp. 539, 541-44.
22. Ibid., pp. 552-56.
23. Ibid., p. 561.
24. Ibid., p. 567.
25. Ibid., p. 579.
26. Ibid., p. 580.
27. Ibid., p. 580.
28. Ibid., p. 581.
29. Roberts, *A Comprehensive History,* 3:386.
30. Ibid., p. 386.
31. Ibid., 4:13.
32. Ibid., p. 15.
33. Ibid., p. 15.
34. Letter of David H. Cannon (President of the St. George Temple). Addressed to President Joseph F. Smith and Counsellors, dated Oct. 21, 1916.
35. *History of the St. George Temple,* Its cost and dedication and Labor thereon (Church Historical Department), pp. 24-25.
36. *History of St. George Temple,* Salt Lake City: Letter of David H. Cannon, p. 25.
37. *Webster's Third New International Dictionary* (unabridged) (Springfield, Mass.: G&C Merriam Co., 1968), p. 750.
38. The *Forum* magazine, Oct. 1927.
39. John 18:37-38.

40. D&C 93:24.
41. *History of the Church*, 5:1-2.
42. *Journal of Discourses*, 2:31 (April 6, 1853).
43. Harold B. Lee, *Decisions for Successful Living* (Salt Lake City: Deseret Book Co., 1973), p. 141; italics added.
44. Talmage, *The House of the Lord*, 1976 ed. rev., p. 84.
45. D&C 124:42.

6

TOGETHER
FOREVER

One Saturday morning I boarded a plane at O'Hare International Airport in Chicago. I was bound for Denver, where, by assignment of the First Presidency, I was to attend the meetings of a stake conference to promote the home teaching program.

The plane made a stop at one of the midwestern cities en route, and an attractive young lady boarded the plane and settled herself in the seat next to mine. She was carrying a rather large white box, obviously intended for carrying clothing. I helped her find a place for it, and we exchanged the usual pleasantries. We were soon engaged in an interesting conversation.

She could not keep the secret in that box very long. It concealed a wedding dress. Happily, excitedly, she told me she was engaged to marry a musician who played in a name band on the Atlantic Coast. The wedding date was set; he would join her in Denver in a few days, and they would marry there.

"So you are being married in Denver," I said, with a question mark in my voice.

"Yes, we are," was the quick reply.

I continued, "It's too bad you can't go over the mountain for your marriage."

"Over the mountain?" she repeated.

"Yes," I said, "in Denver you can be married for this life only. But over the mountain you could be married for this life and for all eternity."

The idea was new and exciting. The conversation went on and on and changed from marriage to Joseph Smith and the Book of Mormon. I had only one copy of the book with me; it was part of the triple combination scripture set, was well worn and marked, and was a gift from a dear friend. I promised to send her a Book of Mormon for a wedding present.

We finally landed in Denver where her parents received her into their arms, and I was met by a stake officer and taken to the conference meetings.

That night as I lay in bed and the experiences of the day passed through my mind, the great contrast between the approaching marriage of this young non-Mormon couple and the marriage available to Latter-day Saints "over the mountain" occupied my thoughts.

Jasmine and I had become engaged in Chicago in the early 1930s, when the nation was suffering from what the Chicagoan called "a slump in the depression." I had worked and saved for more than a year to accumulate enough money for us to go to Salt Lake for our marriage.

In memory I recalled a beautiful sealing room, just off the celestial room, in the Salt Lake Temple; the altar at which we, clothed in the white robes of the temple, kneeled while a servant of God, who was empowered to bind on earth and in heaven, performed the marriage ceremony. I recalled the thrill we both experienced as we heard him say, "For time and for all eternity." As I now thought of the differences between our marriage and the civil marriages I had myself performed and witnessed, and as I considered how much we would have missed in a marriage out of the temple, a deep sense of appreciation and satisfaction filled my heart.

Upon my return to Chicago, I sent the young lady the promised wedding present. Sequel? I don't yet know. I do know that I have always been grateful we went "over the mountain" for our marriage.

Sitting at my desk in the temple annex one morning, I looked out across the lawn at the six-spired stone building known as the temple proper. My eyes quickly covered the familiar scene, from the gold-leafed angel with his eastward pointed trumpet on the highest spire, symbolically proclaiming the restoration of the everlasting gospel to the world, to the largest granite stones at the temple base.

I noticed the carved stone replicas of the sun, the moon, and the stars, symbolizing the three kingdoms of heaven. I thought of the small carved stone images, in appearance like raindrops, on the east side of the temple, symbolic of rays of "living light" descending upon the world. I saw people walking by, intermittently pausing to look up at this amazingly beautiful building. To millions upon millions of tourists from all over the world, and to countless television viewers, this building is a familiar sight. Probably no other building in the world is so well known and so little understood as the Salt Lake Temple.

Externally, it is familiar; internally, it is unknown, except to the Latter-day Saint who has received the great blessings bestowed there. For instance, what does the world know about the sacred ordinance of eternal or celestial marriage? Practically nothing, until it comes into contact with the restored gospel.

One evening, upon invitation of a Jewish Rabbi, I delivered a lecture in a Jewish temple in Chicago. While it was understood that the general subject of the lecture would be "Mormonism," I had, in a preliminary conversation with the Rabbi, agreed to specifically include the matter of "Marriage and the Mormon Family."

As I looked out over the audience, I decided I had better lay some common ground and establish friendship before dealing with our differences. "It may interest you to know that the Mormons and the Jews claim a common ancestry in Abraham, Isaac, and Jacob," I began. "You trace your lineage to Jacob primarily through Judah, whereas we claim family membership chiefly through Joseph.

"You will recall that your ancestor, Judah, sold my ancestor into slavery and that Joseph later repaid Judah by delivering him and the rest of Jacob's posterity from famine. For a time thereafter our families were more or less united, held together by persecution and other external pressures and by a common religion and a belief in Jehovah. However, differences eventually arose, and a second and more lasting separation followed.

"But still, we have had many things in common through the years. We have been about equally popular in the world; we both have practiced for a time a marriage principle which was less than approved by our neighbors; we have given to the world its most valuable literature—the Jews giving the world the holy Bible, referred to by the prophet Ezekiel as 'the stick of Judah'[1] and the descendants of Joseph giving the world their own sacred record—the Book of Mormon, a record of God's dealings with the descendants of Joseph on this continent, also referred to by Ezekiel as 'the stick of Ephraim.'[2] Our peoples share the promise of God that these two records shall one day be joined together as one, and that the peoples who, under the inspiration of God, produced and preserved these records, shall also become one people and have one king—the Lord Jehovah."[3]

Having now established what I felt was a friendly relationship and having aroused curiosity and interest, I proceeded with a discussion of Mormon doctrine, dealing primarily with eternal marriage and the eternal family. When the lecture was ended, men stood up all over the temple to ask questions, almost all of which related to marriage and the family. When the time allotted for questions was up and the last question had been answered, the meeting was adjourned.

After shaking hands with many of the audience, some of whom were friends and acquaintances of mine in the legal profession, I was about to leave when the Rabbi asked if he could detain me a little longer. We sat together, and he said he would like to know more about marriage in the Mormon temple.

"What does the Mormon marriage consist of—what words do you use in the ceremony?"

"I cannot give you the exact words," I replied, "but I can

give you the chief distinction between the Mormon and other marriage ceremonies. It lies in the authority by which the ordinance is performed and the duration of the relationship.

"Marriages outside the temple of God may properly be referred to as civil marriages, the authority and requirements for which are established by the laws of earthly legislatures and governments. The officiators at these marriages may be justices of the peace, judges, sea captains, clergymen of any or all religions, and others too numerous to mention.

"There is no requirement that they have faith in what they are doing, or belief in God, or belief in life after death. The parties entering into the relationship enter into contractual obligations, called covenants, for the period of their mutual lives, with the spectre of death always looming before them as the end of the relationship.

"While meeting the requirements of the civil law of the jurisdiction where the marriage is performed, marriage in a Mormon temple is a higher order of the marital relationship. Death is not mentioned, since death is not the end of the marriage. The contracting parties do not enter into their covenants with a termination in mind. No thought of marriage for the period of their mortal lives only, no thought of death parting them, no mere earthly relationship, enters their minds.

"An officiator, holding the holy Melchizedek Priesthood—the priesthood after the order of the Son of God—an officiator who has been given the power and authority of God to bind and seal in heaven what is being bound and sealed on earth, solemnly pronounces the couple kneeling at the temple altar 'husband and wife, for time and for all eternity' and then bestows upon them blessings revealed of heaven, never heard in any purely earthly ceremony. Children born of such a marriage are, without further act or ordinance, part of an eternal family which, provided both parents and children prove worthy, will survive the grave and continue forever."

The Rabbi's questions were answered; a momentary pause followed: Then he responded in words I shall not soon forget. "That," he said, "is the most appealing religious doctrine I have ever heard; it is the most beautiful concept that has ever entered my mind."

The response of the Rabbi to the concept that marriage and the family can survive the grave and exist eternally was not unique. During my professional life and my many years of service in four missions, I have discussed the subject of eternal marriage and the eternal family with literally thousands of non-Mormons. As they came to understand, at least in part, this doctrine of marriage and the family in eternity, the response, though expressed in various ways, was almost invariably the same as the Rabbi's. A typical expression was "Oh, Mr. Edmunds, that's too good to be true." I always responded, "No, that is not too good to be true; it is just good enough to be true, because it comes from God."

It would seem that all Christians could agree that the first marriage relationship entered into on this earth was performed by God in a garden "eastward in Eden."[4] We have no record of the words used in the ceremony. The scripture simply states that after God created Adam, he said, "It is not good that the man should be alone; I will make him an help meet for him," and the Lord God "made . . . a woman, and brought her unto the man."[5]

When Adam received her, he said, "This is now bone of my bones, and flesh of my flesh: she shall be called Woman, because she was taken out of Man. Therefore shall a man leave his father and his mother, and shall cleave unto his wife: and they shall be one flesh."[6]

For what period of time were they to be united as one? The record is silent. But how could this first marriage have been entered into by Adam and Eve for the period of mortal life when their lives were not mortal until after their transgression and fall? How could death be the foreseeable end of their marriage when death had not entered the world? God's statement "It is not good that man should be alone" was evidently not limited to this life, and "neither is the man without the woman, neither the woman without the man"[7] in the plans of him who created them male and female.

How can we account for the fact that the Mormon philosophy and doctrine with respect to marriage and the eternal family, appealing as it is, has not been a part of the belief and practice of other religions or peoples? It is due to the lack of specific coverage of the doctrine in the scripture to which the world has been limited.

As a result of misunderstanding the scriptures, the Christian world for centuries has been teaching men that there can be no continuation of marriage or family relationships beyond the grave, that all family ties must end with death, and that all the sons and daughters of God will be single forever thereafter. And, if they chance to go to heaven, they will presumably be happy.

Such a fate for his children is not worthy of God. What would heaven be to a man without the eternal companionship of a lovely, loving wife and companion? What sorrow would heaven bestow upon us if the beautiful ties of family were forever ended? Cicero queried, "What gift has Providence bestowed on man that is so dear to him as his children?"[8] No parents, no children, no husband, no wife—what a heaven!

The scripture usually adduced by those who feel that heaven will not have family ties is involved in the case, probably hypothetical, which certain hypocritical Sadducees, who denied the reality of a resurrection, nevertheless presented to Jesus in an effort to entrap him. Matthew records it as follows:

> Master, Moses said, If a man die, having no children, his brother shall marry his wife, and raise up seed unto his brother.
>
> Now there were with us seven brethren: and the first, when he had married a wife, deceased, and, having no issue, left his wife unto his brother:
>
> Likewise the second also, and the third, unto the seventh.
>
> And last of all the woman died also.
>
> Therefore in the resurrection whose wife shall she be of the seven? for they all had her.
>
> Jesus answered and said unto them, Ye do err, not knowing the scriptures, nor the power of God.
>
> For in the resurrection they neither marry, nor are given in marriage, but are as the angels of God in heaven.[9]

Properly understood, Christ's response to this crafty attempt to trap him cannot be considered as authority for the doctrine that all family ties are severed by death. He offered no explanation of his brief reply, since he was not conversing with honest truthseekers.

Marriage for eternity, like baptism, is an ordinance that may not be entered into or performed after the resurrection. The very question asked by the Sadducees evidences a general understanding and belief among the Jews that the woman would or could be the wife of one of the seven brothers in eternity.

There is another important implication in the case. Why should Moses direct that where a married man dies without issue, his brother should marry the widow "and raise up seed unto his (deceased) brother" if the dead brother could have no claim upon or ties with the children in the eternal world? Is there not something more significant in Moses' instruction than the mere perpetuation of the man's name on earth? If the Sadducees had understood the scriptures, they would have known that the brother who could claim the woman as his wife in the resurrection would be the one, if any, to whom she had been authoritatively sealed in marriage for eternity.

Having given to certain of his servants the power and authority that whatsoever they shall bind on earth shall be bound in heaven, would God exclude therefrom the privilege of binding wives to husbands and children to parents, so as to form eternal family relationships? To what higher or more beautiful or important use could the binding authority be put?

Provided both husband and wife observe and keep the covenants of righteousness they make in the temple, celestial or temple marriage not only unites them for eternity but also automatically seals to them the children born of their marriage.

The Lord has also provided for other sealings in his house for those who previously have been married outside the temple. Each year thousands of happily married couples from all parts of world, many of them new converts, come to

88

the holy temples of God to have the sweet marriage relationships into which they had previously entered under secular law and authority extended into eternity by that divine authority which binds on earth and in heaven. Many of them bring their sons and daughters to be sealed to them in an everlasting family relationship for eternity, thus creating an eternal family unit, which to Latter-day Saints is the most important unit in time and in eternity.

I would like to share with you a few lines from a letter which I received several years ago from a convert couple from the state of Washington who had recently received their sealing blessings.

> Dear President Edmunds,
> Just a note of appreciation for your time and care November 2nd, in sealing our family. It is such a beautiful and natural principle that it was surely a strong influence in each of our conversions to the gospel. From the beginning we felt that our marriage should be forever, but did not know it was possible.
> Your words of counsel were of real value and we probably took more heed after 26 years of marriage than we would have as newlyweds. Already their wisdom is evident as we both try harder to go the 100%; and there is a new gentleness in our home. We learned and grew in many ways that evening.
> The only thing that made it at all short of perfect was not having our son with us. However, a return trip to the Temple will be a splendid way to welcome him home from a mission and celebrate a one-year anniversary at the same time!

These sealings, performed only in the temple, are available to all who will accept and live the gospel and thus prove worthy to receive their temple blessings. The sealings are not limited to the living. Through vicarious service, the sacred ordinances of eternal marriage and the sealing of children to parents are extended to the dead, even as is baptism.

By what means did The Church of Jesus Christ of Latter-day Saints come into possession of this most beautiful and transcendently important knowledge that marriage and the family unit can be made to survive the grave and become endless and eternal? Was it by biblical analysis and discovery?

Man may reason and conclude that marriage will survive death from the circumstances surrounding the world's first marriage, or from the statement of Paul that "neither is the man without the woman, neither the woman without the man, in the Lord,"[10] or from his statement that "the husband is the head of the wife, even as Christ is the head of church,"[11] and, without doubt, Christ is the head of the Church eternally. One may reason, too, that the wisdom and love of God would not permit such a beautiful relationship as marriage and family to be ended with death; otherwise, heaven may offer less than earth to the children of God.

The knowledge and doctrine that the marriage relationship may be forever, provided the requirements of obedience and worthiness are met and the marriage be sealed by one possessing the holy priesthood of God, came by revelation of Jesus Christ to the Prophet Joseph Smith at Nauvoo, Illinois, July 12, 1843. In this revelation, the Lord made it clear that all those and only those who make a covenant in marriage with each other "for time and for all eternity," by and under the law of God, and are sealed by a duly appointed servant of God, who has received the holy priesthood and the power to seal on earth and in heaven, shall have an eternally enduring marriage and an eternal family.[12] No other form of marriage will have any effect beyond this life, for the Lord has spoken it clearly:

> Therefore, if a man marry him a wife in the world, and he marry her not by me nor by my word, and he covenant with her so long as he is in the world and she with him, their covenant and marriage are not of force when they are dead, and when they are out of the world; therefore, they are not bound by any law when they are out of the world.
>
> Therefore, when they are out of the world they neither marry nor are given in marriage; but are appointed angels in heaven, which angels are ministering servants, to minister for those who are worthy of a far more, and an exceeding, and an eternal weight of glory.[13]

In inspired instruction the Prophet Joseph says:

> In the celestial glory there are three heavens or degrees;
> And in order to obtain the highest, a man must enter into

this order of the priesthood (meaning the new and everlasting covenant of marriage);
And if he does not, he cannot obtain it.
He may enter into the other, but that is the end of his kingdom; he cannot have an increase.[14]

This means that even though a man or woman shall live worthy of the celestial kingdom and dwell in the presence of God, the Father, neither he nor she can obtain a fulness of glory without the blessing of an eternal marriage.

With eternal glory riding on the choice, what Latter-day Saint girl or boy, man or woman, will chance a marriage outside the Church, outside the temple, outside the law of God! And yet, many do.

I recall the case of a Mormon girl married to a Catholic boy. After the marriage, she continued to affiliate with her church and he with his. No major marriage problems arose between them until the birth of their first child. He wanted the child baptized in the Catholic Church immediately to ensure its being saved. She insisted that no innocent child would be lost by its failure to be baptized in infancy. He prevailed.

Disagreement followed disagreement with respect to the religious training and upbringing of the child. Finally, in desperation, they both came to me with their problem. After listening to their troubles, I asked why they had married outside their respective faiths.

She replied, "I thought he would love me enough to join our church after we were married." He responded immediately, "And I thought she would become Catholic."

I gave them the best advice I could, but, at this point, the best is seldom good enough. The best advice precedes marriage and is the advice given by the Lord to marry according to his word, which is his law, by his authority, and in the place he has appointed—his holy temple. I echo the words of Brigham Young:

> There is not a young man in our community who would not be willing to travel from here to England to be married right, if he understood things as they are; there is not a young woman in our community, who loves the Gospel and wishes

its blessings, that would be married in any other way; they would live unmarried until they could be married as they should be, if they lived until they were as old as Sarah before she had Isaac born to her. Many of our brethren have married off their children without taking this into consideration, and thinking it a matter of little importance. I wish we all understood this in the light in which heaven understands it.[15]

NOTES

1. Ezekiel 37:16-20.
2. Ibid. 37:16-20; see also 2 Nephi 3:7, 11-12.
3. Ibid. 37:21-22, 27-28.
4. Genesis 2:8.
5. Genesis 2:18, 21-22.
6. Genesis 2:23-24.
7. 1 Corinthians 11:11.
8. *The International Dictionary of Thoughts* (Chicago: J.G. Ferguson Publishing Company, 1969), p. 126.
9. Matthew 22:23-30.
10. 1 Corinthians 11:11.
11. Ephesians 5:23.
12. D&C 132:19.
13. D&C 132:15-16.
14. D&C 131:1-4.
15. Widtsoe, *Discourses of Brigham Young,* pp. 195-96.

7

THE FOREVER FAMILY

I had been invited by a fine Latter-day Saint couple to officiate in the sealing of an adopted child to them in the Salt Lake Temple. I had performed many such sealings, but this one was special. The child was a beautiful five-year-old girl with sparkling black eyes. She had been born in South America to parents plagued by poverty. At the age of seven months the child was suffering from malnutrition and bronchial pneumonia. For this and other inexplicable reasons, unknown to me, the parents decided not to keep the child and planned to end the child's life by burning her in a fire made of wood and animal fat.

Why a father and mother should choose such a cruel, inhumane means of ridding themselves of an unwanted child is beyond my comprehension. An outside fire was kindled, the child was placed in it, and the hot oil began spattering over the defenseless little body. The screams of the child attracted the attention of a policeman passing by, and the child was rescued before the burning became fatal.

The child was placed in an orphanage, where she spent the next two years. The hot oil had left scars on her body, but her face was clear except for a scar on the left lower cheek. It was this scar that drew my attention and led the adoptive parents to relate the story.

The adoptive parents had heard of the child through a doctor who had visited the orphanage. Their hearts went out to the little one; they made inquiry as to the possibility of adopting the child and giving her a good home where love and kindness might compensate for such a tragic beginning to life. The adoption was arranged, and the little girl was brought by loving parents to the United States. The child was now five years old, and plastic surgery had removed much of the apparent damage of the burning.

There was more than the usual interest and emotion in the sealing room that morning. Friends and relatives sat with tear-filled eyes listening to the sacred ceremony which sealed a little girl to loving adoptive parents for time and all eternity, bestowing upon her all the rights and blessings that a child born in the covenant would possess.

The ordinance was completed; the parents could hardly wait to take the little one, now their own for eternity, into their arms. The child, having been well taught by these parents, seemed to sense the importance of the ordinance to her and embraced her father and mother with an extra measure of appreciation and joy.

I completed the sealing sheet which now bore record that I had officiated in the performance of the sacred ordinance, and returned it to the sealing office on the third floor of the temple. Having done this, I entered the elevator to return to my office. The elevator stopped on the second floor, where the sealing had taken place, and the child entered the elevator along with a sister temple worker who was accompanying the child to the children's waiting room, where she would exchange the white temple clothing for her own clothing and her parents would call for her.

Upon seeing me, the child's face lighted up, and she immediately began talking. It was no idle chatter. It was an amazing demonstration of comprehension of what had occurred. Looking up at me with those beautiful eyes, half assertively, half quizzically, she said, "My mother forever, my mother forever, my mother forever."

Assertion or question, it mattered not. I responded, "Yes, my dear, *your mother forever*." She was satisfied. At last she had a real mother with a mother's love, and *forever*.

All the day those words rang in my ears, "My mother forever," and I seemed to have a deeper appreciation for the sealing ordinances which a wise and merciful Creator had provided for his faithful children—ordinances which bound children and parents together in an eternal family relationship. I had a new appreciation for the message which Moroni, once a warrior and prophet on the American continent and later a resurrected, glorified being, brought from heaven to Joseph Smith in the upper room of the humble farm house of the Smith family near Palmyra, New York, on that memorable night of September 21, 1823.

The instruction from God, sent through his angel, Moroni, covered a variety of subjects, an explanation of many little understood prophecies of the Old and New Testaments and other instruction intended to prepare Joseph Smith for his divine mission and calling as the first and great prophet of the final dispensation of the gospel on this earth. Concerning one of the most important and interesting parts of the message brought by Moroni, Joseph writes:

> He first quoted part of the third chapter of Malachi; and he quoted also the fourth or last chapter of the same prophecy, though with a little variation from the way it reads in our Bibles. Instead of quoting the first verse as it reads in our books, he quoted it thus:
> *For behold, the day cometh that shall burn as an oven, and all the proud, yea, and all that do wickedly shall burn as stubble; for they that come shall burn them, saith the Lord of Hosts, that it shall leave them neither root nor branch.*
> And again, he quoted the fifth verse thus:
> *Behold, I will reveal unto you the Priesthood, by the hand of Elijah the prophet, before the coming of the great and dreadful day of the Lord.*
> He also quoted the next verse differently:
> *And he shall plant in the hearts of the children the promises made to the fathers, and the hearts of the children shall turn to their fathers. If it were not so, the whole earth would be utterly wasted at his coming.* [1]

Moroni's variation of the words of Malachi, appearing in the last chapter of the Old Testament, adds some exceedingly interesting and important dimensions to Malachi's prophecy. The first of these new dimensions is contained in the words, "Behold, I will *reveal unto you the priesthood*, by the hand of Elijah the prophet." What is meant by "reveal the Priesthood"?

When, in fulfillment of the prophetic promise, Elijah appeared to Joseph Smith and Oliver Cowdery in the Kirtland Temple in 1836, what did he bestow upon them that they had not received before? They had received the holy priesthood seven years earlier under the hands of Peter, James, and John and had been ordained Apostles. What could Elijah add to this? The Savior himself had conferred the holy priesthood upon Peter, James, and John and had ordained them Apostles; but it was left for Elijah, under the direction of Christ, to confer the sealing keys, powers, and authority upon them on the Mount of Transfiguration.

Likewise, in this final dispensation, though the priesthood and apostleship had been conferred upon Joseph Smith and Oliver Cowdery by Peter, James, and John, it was left to the same great prophet, Elijah, to confer upon them the knowledge and keys of the sealing powers of the priesthood which he held. He brought to them a *revelation* of the sealing authority, power, and blessings of the holy priesthood—the authority and power to seal wives to husbands, children to parents—blessings pertaining to both living and dead.

This, then, is what was meant by the promise, "I will reveal unto you the Priesthood": it was to make known the purposes, powers, and blessings of the priesthood, the knowledge of which Joseph and Oliver had not received nor comprehended before then.

Prior to the coming of Elijah there had been no eternal marriages performed in the Church for the living, and there had been neither baptisms nor sealings performed in behalf of the dead. It was Elijah who gave to Joseph Smith and Oliver Cowdery this expanded knowledge of the powers and blessings of the priesthood and the keys and authority to implement the great sealing work for the blessing of living and dead. As he did so, he said, "The keys of this dispensation are committed into your hands."[2]

There is still another new dimension of light and truth in the words of the Lord to Joseph Smith, through Moroni, on that memorable night in 1823 when, referring to Elijah's mission, he said:

> And he shall plant in the hearts of the children the promises made to the fathers, and the hearts of the children shall turn to their fathers.

Just what were the "promises made to the fathers" and who made the promises? The promises referred to are at least two-fold. First, the promises made to the fathers in the great council of our Eternal Father and his spirit children convened in heaven before the earth was formed: there God presented to his children his plan for their mortality and for their salvation and exaltation.

An earth would be created, and in God's appointed time each of his spirit children would be sent to earth to receive a mortal body, to undergo the experiences of mortal life with its joys and sorrows, and to be tested and proved to see if he and she would "do all things whatsoever the Lord their God shall command them."[3]

The many noble and great among our Father's spirit children would become the leaders and rulers in his earthly kingdom. Abraham was singled out as one of the noble and great.[4] Michael would come to earth first and be known as Adam and would, with his companion, Eve, become the parents of the Father's mortal family on earth. Through transgression, they would bring death into the world—a death required for immortality and eternal life. Jehovah, the Firstborn of God's spirit children, would atone for the transgression of our first parents, make possible the forgiveness of man's own sins upon condition of full repentance, and provide for his salvation and exaltation through his obedience to the laws and ordinances of the gospel.

There would be periods of time when, because of apostasy, the gospel would not be available to man on earth and many would, through no fault of their own, live and die without the knowledge and ordinances of the gospel. How could they be compensated for this great loss? Well, they were given the promise and assurance that the gospel would be taught to them in the spirit world after death and that their children who were appointed to come to earth when the gospel in its fulness could be received by them would perform the saving and exalting priesthood ordinances, by proxy, in their behalf. These were the promises made by God and, undoubtedly, also by the children to the fathers. With this understanding, "All the sons of God shouted for joy"[5] when the foundations of the earth were laid.

The fact that we do not recall our premortal life and "the promises made to the fathers" is not important. The promises were made, and the children are obligated to keep them. With the coming of Elijah with the keys to perform the ordinances, there were planted in the hearts of the children "the promises made to the fathers." By faith the promises are recognized and accepted by the children, and by faith the hearts of the children turn to their fathers and they keep and fulfill those promises.

The "promises made to the fathers" may have another dimension: they may include the promises made by God to Father Abraham during his life and confirmed upon his son, Isaac, and grandson, Jacob, to the effect that through Abraham and his seed all the families of the earth should receive the blessings of the gospel. Abraham records the great promises made to him in these words:

> My name is Jehovah, and I know the end from the beginning; therefore my hand shall be over thee.
>
> And I will make of thee a great nation, and I will bless thee above measure, and make thy name great among all nations, and thou shalt be a blessing unto thy seed after thee, that in their hands they shall bear this ministry and Priesthood unto all nations;
>
> And I will bless them through thy name; for as many as receive this Gospel shall be called after thy name, and *shall be accounted thy seed*, and shall rise up and bless thee, as their father;
>
> And I will bless them that bless thee, and curse them that curse thee; and in thee *(that is, in thy Priesthood)* and in thy seed *(that is,* thy Priesthood), for I give unto thee a *promise* that this right shall continue in thee, and in thy seed after thee (that is to say, the literal seed, or the seed of the body)

shall all the families of the earth be blessed, even with the blessings of the Gospel, which are the blessings of salvation, even of life eternal.[6]

Here, then, are other "promises made to the fathers"—promises that through them and their seed, by the priesthood, all the families of the earth would be blessed with "the blessings of salvation, even of life eternal." The words "all the families of the earth" surely are not restricted to the comparative few who hear and accept the gospel on earth, but rather include *all* families, living and dead, who have lived upon the earth.

Should not these promises be planted in the hearts of the children of the fathers—Abraham, Isaac, and Jacob? Should not the children appreciate these promises made to their fathers? Should not their hearts turn to their fathers in gratitude? Should not they perform the mission given them to bless all men, living and dead, by giving unto them the gospel, with the blessings of salvation and life eternal? By the exercise of the sealing authority and power of the priesthood the seed of Abraham are now carrying the gospel to the families of the earth and are performing the sacred ordinances of the priesthood in the temples of God in behalf of the dead.

I must not conclude this chapter on "The Forever Family" without reference to a brilliant discourse delivered by one of the great leaders of this dispensation, Elder George Q. Cannon, who served as counselor to Presidents Brigham Young, John Taylor, Wilford Woodruff, and Lorenzo Snow. Speaking on the subject of temples and temple ordinances on April 8, 1871, in the Salt Lake Tabernacle, he said:

> We are born on the earth, where family relationships that are most desirable are formed. Parents have their children whom they love beyond expression. These children grow up and form associations in life and raise families, and these relationships are the most tender known to the human heart. There is nothing so much calculated to make life desirable as the relation of parents to children and children to parents, husbands to wives and wives to husbands; and many a man when he loses his partner, loses all the hope that he has; his heart sinks within him, and he feels as if life was undesirable; and instances are not rare of men, through grief on this

account, having their lives shortened. And so with the other sex; sometimes through the loss of a husband a woman's heart will break and she goes down to an early grave. And yet, in the midst of the world where all these tender ties and emotions exist there is no preparation for their perpetuation. . . . Imagine, if you can, a state of things where all these relationships are utterly destroyed and all mingle in one common herd! This is the kind of heaven that many people believe they are going to. I have heard ministers say, "I will not know any relationship between myself and my wife hereafter; she, then, will be no nearer to me than any other woman, nor I to her than any other man; our children will be no nearer to us than any other children, and we will live in this condition throughout the endless ages of eternity." This is a dreary prospect for any human being who has the affection of a husband, wife, parent or child—a dreary prospect for that endless eternity to which we are all hastening.[7]

Then Elder Cannon went on to describe the heaven to which the Latter-day Saints look forward:

It is not a heaven where all distinctions are abolished— where parents and children are mingled with the common mass, where wives and husbands are undistinguishable; but where all these ties exist and are preserved and perpetuated, and man goes forward on that heavenly career which God, his Heavenly Father, has assigned to him, and which he designs that all his faithful children shall walk in. These are some of the reasons why we want a temple built.[8]

Moroni's greatest message with respect to the mission of the Prophet Elijah was that he would reveal anew the purposes, powers, and blessings of the holy priesthood that had long been lost to the world; he would restore the great sealing power of the priesthood; he would restore the keys to implement the work, the purposes, and powers of the priesthood; and he would plant in the hearts of the children the desire and motivation to extend the blessings of the sealing powers and ordinances of the priesthood to their fathers, according to the promises that had been made to the fathers.

Through the sealing power and authority restored by Elijah, the sweet and sacred relationships of mortality may be extended into immortality, and the families of the earth may become the families of heaven—forever and eternal families. Through the sealing power restored through Elijah that sweet child from South America was bound and sealed into a family where she was loved and wanted, for time and for all eternity —*an eternal family—a forever family.*

NOTES

1. Joseph Smith 2:37-39.
2. D&C 110:16.
3. Abraham 3:24-25.
4. Abraham 3:23.
5. Job 38:4, 7.
6. Abraham 2:8-11; italics added.
7. *Journal of Discourses,* 14:127.
9. *Journal of Discourses,* 14:129

8

OBLIGATION
OR OPPORTUNITY

A chemistry professor came into our Chicago law offices one day for the purpose of having me draft a will. He was a bachelor in his sixties and had no family relationships nearer than cousins. While his estate would be a modest one, he desired it to be distributed according to his intentions rather than leave it to the law and the courts to make the determination as to who should inherit his property upon his death. I soon made a list of his assets and his relatives and the portion of his estate each one was to receive.

I was ready to terminate the conference when he said to me, "I have something else, Mr. Edmunds, which to me is more valuable than any of the properties you have on the list, but I can't think of anyone who would want it."

"What is that?" I asked.

"Well, I have, over the years, accumulated a considerable amount of genealogical data on our family. Our earliest family roots in America were in Pennsylvania." He said he was a cousin of the late Martin G. Brumbaugh, a former governor of Pennsylvania and professor of education at the University of Pennsylvania. I had read an excellent book written by Brumbaugh on the art of teaching, and we were soon engaged in an interesting conversation regarding his family.

The records he had accumulated had not been organized. He had given some thought to making a book out of them, but he had not gotten around to it.

An idea began taking shape in my mind. "You are sure none of your family would want those records?" I asked.

"I'm quite sure of it. None of the family has shown any interest whatsoever in them."

"Well," I said, "I can tell you what to do with your records."

"What should I do with them?" he inquired.

"Give them to me."

An expression of curiosity lit up his face as he asked, "What would you do with them?"

"I am a Mormon," I said, "and Mormons have a great interest in genealogical records. We have probably the greatest genealogical library in the world. It is much larger than the Newberry Library here in Chicago. We would be happy to add your records to our library."

Still curious, he asked, "Of what use would my family records be to your church?"

"Oh, your records would be examined and processed. Then the names of all your deceased relatives would be forwarded to the Salt Lake Temple and your relatives would have baptisms performed for them, and they would be made Mormons." The shock was to be expected. He quickly responded, "I don't think I want that done, and I don't think my family would, either."

I then explained to him the plan of salvation for the dead, beginning with the teaching of the gospel to the dead by Christ during the three-day period his body lay lifeless in the tomb,[1] followed by the baptism for the dead recorded by Paul.[2] He appeared to be interested and impressed with this new concept, but he was far from convinced that this temple ordinance should be performed for any of his family. He would have closed the matter by saying, "I think I'd better discuss this with my Cousin Floyd before I make a decision." Cousin Floyd was an editor on the staff of one of Chicago's leading newspapers. I could imagine how he would respond if the matter were presented to him "cold." The proposal would not have a chance of survival, much less acceptance.

I turned the conversation back to his family and the high esteem in which he held it. I explained how that family might become an eternal family with him as an integral part of it. He was now obviously more impressed but still reluctant and undecided.

I pursued the matter a little further. "If the gospel as taught by The Church of Jesus Christ of Latter-day Saints is true," I said, "and is the plan of salvation for all people, both living and dead, and is being taught in the spirit world as well as on earth, don't you think there is a possibility that some of your ancestors could have heard and accepted it already?"

"Well, it is possible, I suppose," he replied.

I continued, "Now, if we can't rule out that possibility, is it not also possible that these family members may be waiting, patiently or impatiently, for someone to perform that necessary ordinance of baptism for them which Paul tells us was performed by the early Christians on behalf of their dead?"

He hedged a bit and was still undecided. I finally explained that the performance of baptism and other temple rites and ordinances for the dead placed the dead under no compulsion to accept those ordinances, that the acceptance of the ordinances is for them not an *obligation* but an *opportunity*. I then asked him if he thought the dead should be permitted to make the choice for themselves or if the living had the right to make the choice for them.

The case was closed. Faced with the decision as to whether his family should have the ordinances of the gospel made available to them by proxy and be permitted to choose for themselves to accept or reject them, or whether he should withhold the ordinances from his kindred, at least temporarily, and thus deprive them of their immediate freedom of choice, he delivered his genealogical records to me without consulting Cousin Floyd. I delivered them to the Genealogical Society of the Church.

It seems that all he needed was the assurance that the

performance of ordinances by proxy in a Mormon temple would not make Mormons of his family members except by their own choosing and that the performance of the ordinances imposed no obligation on his deceased kindred but simply afforded them the opportunity to choose between accepting or rejecting the ordinances. With this understanding, he was willing to let the dead exercise the right to choose.

Admittedly, I did use some persuasion in the case, yet I believe that his decision was a predictable and natural decision to make under the circumstances. I believe that somehow there has been planted in the hearts and minds of men—not just some men but all men—an innate desire for freedom of choice, and, except for a few who for selfish reasons would deprive mankind of this freedom, there is a universal recognition and belief that the right of freedom of choice is the God-given right of all mankind. I am convinced that if a religious creed could be formulated that would even approach acceptance by all men, it would of necessity contain as one of its tenets something similar to our Article of Faith:

> We claim the privilege of worshipping Almighty God according to the dictates of our own conscience, and allow all men the same privilege, let them worship how, where, or what they may.[3]

Freedom to choose and to act upon that choice has been with us from the beginning. It is a right given of God to all his spirit children in the premortal world. In the exercise of this right, Lucifer rebelled against God and became Satan, the devil. In the exercise of it, many of our Father's children followed Lucifer and attempted to force his philosophy of life upon all others. They thereby forfeited the privilege of remaining in heaven and the right to mortality with its blessings. Referring to this, the Lord said:

> Behold, the devil was before Adam, for he rebelled against me, saying, Give me thine honor, which is my power; and also a third part of the hosts of heaven turned he away from me *because of their agency;*

And they were thrust down, and thus came the devil and his angels.[4]

By the perfect use of the right of freedom of choice, Jehovah accepted the appointment offered him as the Firstborn in the spirit and became the Savior and Redeemer of mankind, the "Lamb slain from (before) the foundation of the world."[5] This right of freedom of choice came with man into mortality.

The whole concept of eternal rewards and punishments is based upon the right of freedom of choice. Upon what conceivable theory or premise could man be justly rewarded or punished in the absence of the right to choose his course of action?

Freedom of choice involves the presentation to the mind of multiple alternatives of thought or action in opposition to each other, which we call choices, and the power to accept the one which, at the time, offers the greatest enticement or appeal. There must of necessity be at least two choices. If there were only one choice, then there could be no merit or demerit in our action, and, consequently, no reward or punishment could justly be meted out to us or follow from our action. A great prophet who lived six hundred years before the birth of Christ gave this inspired instruction to his family:

For it must needs be, that there is an opposition in all things. If not so . . . righteousness could not be brought to pass, neither wickedness, neither holiness nor misery, neither good nor bad. . . .

And if ye shall say there is no law, ye shall also say there is no sin. If ye shall say there is no sin, ye shall also say there is no righteousness, and if there be no righteousness there be no happiness. And if there be no righteousness nor happiness there be no punishment nor misery. And if these things are not there is no God. And if there is no God we are not, neither the earth; for there could have been no creation of things, neither to act nor to be acted upon; wherefore, all things must have vanished away.

. . . There is a God, and he hath created all things . . . both things to act and things to be acted upon. . . .

Wherefore, men are free according to the flesh; and all things are given unto them which are expedient unto man. And they are free to choose liberty and eternal life, through the great mediation of all men, or to choose captivity and death, according to the captivity and power of the devil; for he seeketh that all men might be miserable like unto himself.[6]

Here is philosophy worthy of the name, a philosophy of the highest order, and in its most logical form. To have righteousness and happiness, sin and misery, we must start with law. The law referred to comes from God. Righteousness consists in the keeping of the law, and happiness and eternal life are the products thereof. Sin is the transgression of the law and its products are misery and death.

God gives to man "all things which are expedient unto man."[7] All things which are expedient must include (1) the laws of God, (2) the ability to distinguish between good and evil, right and wrong, and (3) the freedom of choice. Having been given the laws of God, man must also be given the light to choose, together with the right to choose.

The prophet Job has said, "There is a spirit in man: and the inspiration of the Almighty giveth them understanding."[8] Christ declared that he is the light of the world[9] which "lighteth every man that cometh into the world."[10] Moroni, the last of the Book of Mormon prophets and the first of the prophets sent from God in this last dispensation, said, "Behold, the Spirit of Christ is given to every man, that he may know good from evil."[11] Having been given the laws of God, the ability to discern what is good and what is evil, and been granted the freedom to choose between them, man becomes a free agent, responsible for his actions, accountable to God.

I recall a telephone conversation with an assistant states attorney for Cook County, Illinois, to whom I had given a copy of the Book of Mormon. "How are you this morning?" I began.

"I'm all right except for the Book of Mormon," he responded.

"What's wrong with the Book of Mormon?" I asked.

"There's nothing wrong with it except that I can't put it down at night. I stay awake all night reading that book and am losing my sleep."

"It is interesting, isn't it?" I said.

He responded: "It is one of the most interesting books I

have ever read. The philosophy in it concerning law and sin and justice, mercy and righteousness and happiness intrigues me. It is profound, and it's true."

"Do you believe the book is true?" I asked.

"Yes, John, I do. The evidence of its truth is in the book itself. You need no other evidence."

By decree of a just God, there is given to all men the right and privilege to hear the gospel and to receive the gospel, either in mortality or after death. And all who will receive the gospel will receive, in person or by proxy, the ordinances of the gospel required for their salvation and exaltation in the presence of the Father. But none will be forced to accept the gospel or any of its ordinances. Man is left free, by decree and gift of God, to choose for himself, or to reject for himself, this plan of salvation. There is absolutely no coercion or force involved in the plan. No man was ever predestined by God to be saved or to be damned.

But the plan—the principles and ordinances by which man is either saved in accepting or damned in rejecting—is "predestined," or, more accurately, "pre-ordained." It is a one-and-only plan.

This plan, however, does not violate the right to freedom of choice. It was not forced upon us nor established without our consent nor contrary to our free choice. In the exercise of our free agency, we accepted the plan in the premortal life, in the grand council in heaven. Having freely accepted the plan, we are consequently irrevocably bound by it. We now may choose to follow the plan or not to follow it, but with the definite understanding that we will, under the plan, be responsible for the results of our choice. The acceptance of the gospel is not and never has been a matter of compulsion or *obligation*. It is, for the living and for the dead alike, a matter of *opportunity*.

NOTES

1. 1 Peter 3:18-20.
2. 1 Corinthians 15:29.
3. Articles of Faith, 11.
4. D&C 29:36-37.
5. Moses 7:47.
6. 2 Nephi 2:11, 13-14, 27.
7. 2 Nephi 2:27.
8. Job 32:8.
9. John 9:5.
10. John 1:9.
11. Moroni 7:16.

9

UNTIL YOU "MAKE IT"

I recall an embarrassing experience that came to me during the early, lean years of my law practice in Chicago. A brother of mine, engaged in the practice of medicine, persisted in giving to me and my wife gifts that were then beyond our financial ability to match or reciprocate. When, at last the "windows opened" and we could afford to send him and his wife a Christmas gift comparable to the gifts we had been receiving, we eagerly went to one of Chicago's famous stores and selected some beautiful china plates.

It was early November, and we did not want the plates mailed until mid-December. We proposed to pay for them and have them held until that time. The clerk explained that it was contrary to store policy to hold merchandise that long after full payment had been made, but that we could make a small payment on account and they would hold the plates until we paid the balance and ordered them sent. We, accordingly, made a small payment on account and left.

Early in December we decided to pay the balance and have the gift sent. We rode together from our suburban home to the central business area of Chicago, called "the Loop"; I proceeded to my law office and my wife went to the store. Shortly after that my telephone rang. It was my wife; she was in the store prepared to pay for the gift and have it sent. She was advised by one of the clerks that the gift had already been mailed.

"How can this be?" she asked. "We were told that it would be held until we paid the balance due on it and ordered it mailed." The clerk checked on the matter again and then told my wife that the gift had been sent out about two weeks earlier, "COD." Horrors! What embarrassment! What would my brother think of me for sending a Christmas gift COD?

Well, I immediately wrote a letter of explanation and apology and enclosed my check to cover the COD charges. The embarrassment seemed to intensify as we awaited his response.

In a few days I received a letter such as only my brother would have written. It went something like this: "We were surprised, John, to receive a Christmas gift from you 'COD.' However, I accepted it at the post office, paid the amount due, and took it home. We opened it and found the exquisitely beautiful plates. We thank you and will certainly make good use of them. I might tell you that we showed the plates to our friends and neighbors and told them how the gift came to us. They all think the giving of Christmas gifts 'COD' is a great idea and are all for bigger and better Christmas gifts. We were already planning on what we would send you next Christmas when your letter arrived." The embarrassment finally ended, and we began to enjoy the experience.

One day while I was reflecting upon this experience, the thought came to me that we might consider our gifts from heaven as coming to us "COD." In any event they must be paid for before we can receive them. This seemed to be the import of the Lord's instruction through Joseph Smith:

> There is a law, irrevocably decreed in heaven before the foundations of this world, upon which all blessings are predicated—
>
> And when we obtain any blessing from God, it is by obedience to that law upon which it is predicated.[1]

The Lord followed this instruction with further instruction to the same effect:

For all who will have a blessing at my hands shall abide the law which was appointed for that blessing, and the conditions thereof, as were instituted from before the foundation of the world.[2]

If these scriptures be correct, we have no charge account in heaven: our gifts and blessings must be paid for before they are received by us, and the price is *obedience* to the laws and commandments of God.

Many Latter-day Saints seem to believe that when they have received the endowment and the eternal marriage ordinance in the temple they "have it made." This, however, is a gross error. As I have officiated in temple marriages, I have, almost invariably, counseled the couples not to go away from the temple and cheat themselves by assuming that they "have it made" and that an eternal marriage is now assured. I counsel them: "You don't have anything made *unless and until you make it* —make it to the end of your lives, observing your covenants and keeping the commandments of God."

As the holy endowment ceremonies of the temple proceed and each promised blessing is pronounced or sealed upon a recipient, that person assumes an obligation or enters into a covenant of obedience, and the promised blessing is contingent upon the faithful observance of the obligation and covenant. Like the endowment, the eternal marriage ordinance and the sealing of wife to husband and children to parents are blessings that are conditioned upon our keeping the covenants made in connection with the ordinances, which entails full compliance with the laws and commandments of God. Brigham Young warned those who fail to keep their covenants:

> We see Latter-day Saints, after traveling five, ten, twenty, and even forty years, faithful in the kingdom of God, turn away from the holy commandments. They will be lost, and all that they have had, and all that they think they have will be taken from them and given to those who are faithful.[3]

The Lord has often declared that "he that endureth to the end shall be saved."[4] These words must not be misunderstood nor considered out of context. "Enduring to the end" does not mean merely tolerating life and its vicissitudes until we die. In each case where the words appear there is a presumption that those to whom the words are directed are "in the way" that leads to salvation. If one is on the road to destruction, obviously there is no salvation in enduring to the end on that course. The parable of the prodigal son is ample authority for the fact that there is no salvation in "riotous living." Salvation comes through "righteous living."

I do not suppose that my COD Christmas gift is likely to set a precedent or that the idea will "catch on" anywhere. Where the receiver of the gift has no choice but to pay and accept, there is neither giving nor generosity. Neither is there any assurance that happiness will result. Disappointment might well become the rule. The Lord's gifts do not deprive the recipient of freedom of choice. The Lord offers the gift, but man is free to accept or reject it. The acceptance price is always "obedience to law." The Lord says:

> For if you will that I give unto you a place in the celestial world, you must prepare yourselves by doing the things which I have commanded you and required of you.[5]

One of the greatest tragedies of life is this—that man chooses to receive so little of what God offers him. I am reminded of Emerson's inspired poem, entitled "Days":

> Daughters of Time, the hypocritic Days,
> Muffled and dumb like barefoot dervishes,
> And walking single in an endless file,
> Bring diadems and fagots in their hands.
> To each they offer gifts after his will,
> Bread, kingdom, stars, and sky that holds them all.
> I, in my pleachéd garden, watched the pomp,
> Forgot my morning wishes, hastily
> Took a few herbs and apples, and the Day
> Turned and departed silent. I, too late,
> Under her solemn fillet saw the scorn.[6]

Why is it that when the Lord invites us to the feast we choose to eat but a few crumbs from his table? Why is it that when he offers us the holy endowment and an eternal marriage ordinance in his house less than half of the Latter-day Saint couples prepare themselves to accept his offer? Why do the majority of Latter-day Saint couples fail to qualify themselves to accept the Lord's offer or choose rather a civil marriage with no promise or obligation beyond the grave?

Perhaps the answer lies in a lack of understanding of God's plan for the eternal happiness of his children. President Spencer W. Kimball has given the following counsel to the youth of the Church, which is equally applicable to all Latter-day Saints who are contemplating marriage:

> Our youth often ask the vital question: "Whom shall I marry?" The proper answer to that question brings a proper answer to many others. If you marry the proper "whom," you are sure to marry in the proper "where," and you have an infinitely better chance of happiness here and in eternity.[7]

Speaking at a Regional Representatives seminar held in conjunction with the 146th semiannual conference (reported in the *Church News* October 23, 1976, p. 5) President Spencer W. Kimball expressed concern for those who are marrying outside the temple. He said:

> We can never be happy with less than 50 percent of our people marrying in the temple. That is terrifying to me to think that more than half of our boys and girls are marrying outside the temple when there are temples available to practically everyone in the Church.

Brigham Young adds this caveat:

> Do not marry unbelievers—Be careful, O ye mothers of Israel, and do not teach your daughters in [the] future, as many of them have been taught, to marry out of Israel. Woe to you who do it; you will lose your crowns as sure as God lives.[8]

Not understanding God's plan of life, we establish unwise priorities and pursue them to the bitter end. In giving final counsel to our California missionaries at the termination of their missions, I always advised them that they must choose between quantity and quality in the selection of their priorities. "The quantity of life," I said, "consists in its length of years. The quality of your life will be determined by your priorities; and the highest priorities ever established were announced by the Master when he said to his disciples, 'Seek ye first the kingdom of God, and his righteousness.' "[9]

The Lord gave us an insight into priorities in an incomparable revelation on priesthood and its uses and blessings.

He distinguished between the "chosen" and the "called." The chosen were those who so magnified their callings and opportunities that God chose them to receive his greatest blessings in time and in eternity. These blessings were stated, as follows:

> . . . Then shall thy confidence wax strong in the presence of God; and the doctrine of the priesthood shall distil upon thy soul as the dews from heaven.
>
> The Holy Ghost shall be thy constant companion, and thy scepter an unchanging scepter of righteousness and truth; and thy dominion shall be an everlasting dominion, and without compulsory means it shall flow unto thee forever and ever.[10]

In this revelation God further declared, "There are many called, but few are chosen," and then he proceeds to ask, "And why are they not chosen?" He continues with the answer: *"Because their hearts are set so much upon the things of this world, and aspire to the honors of men."*[11]

It is a case of priorities, is it not? And the disposition of men to act foolishly in the choice of life's priorities is as prevalent today as it was when this revelation was given. Numberless are the men, and women, too, who seek first the riches of this world and the honors of men and who measure the success of their lives by these acquisitions.

It has been said that "wealth is a superfluity of the things we don't need." I recall such a superfluity being strikingly evidenced at an auction sale of the wardrobe of a wealthy Chicago woman after her death. It required three days to auction off her wardrobe which included, among other things: 500 cloth coats, 24 fur pieces, 1,000 daytime dresses, 1,000 purses and 1,500 pairs of shoes. If she had worn two different pairs of shoes each day, it would have taken her nearly two years to wear each pair once. Need we seek a better example of "a superfluity of things we do not need"?

I had concluded a business discussion with an officer of one of Chicago's great banks. He was in the top echelon of the bank staff. We had arisen from our chairs, and I was about to leave when he said: "I may not see you again, John.

I will reach mandatory retirement age in a few days and will be leaving the bank."

I thought I detected a note of sadness in his voice. He beckoned to another officer and said to me, "I want you to get acquainted with my successor." We were immediately joined by the other officer. Introducing us, he said to the other officer, "Mr. Edmunds is a valued customer of this bank, and I want to make sure that after I leave he will be given all the consideration and courtesy he has a right to expect."

I interrupted him, saying, "I may not be able to do business with the bank much longer, Tom; I am retiring myself."

"You mean you are closing your law practice, John?" he asked.

"Yes, at least temporarily," I replied.

"Why? What are you going to do?" he asked.

"Well, I am going to California to serve as a Mormon missionary for the next three years," I said.

A look of sheer incredulity came into Tom's face and he was silent for a minute. Then his expression seemed to change and, taking hold of my arm and the arm of his successor, he drew us close to him and began talking. Possibly he was just thinking aloud, as he said something like this:

"Don't interrupt me; I want to express a few thoughts that have come to me lately. To realize that I have reached the age of retirement has proved quite a shock to me. It has caused me to do some serious thinking of life and what it's all about. I started life as a poor boy. My father died without leaving me a penny. I worked at one job and another until I was employed by this bank. I have worked hard and have come up through the ranks to the position I now hold.

"I can retire and travel or do any of the other things I have always thought I would like to do. The bank's been good to me; I am financially independent. I have no money worries whatsoever; I'm well fixed for the rest of my life. But as I have reflected on my life, I have seriously wondered of what worth, if any, my life has really been to anyone other than my family and myself.

"Now, John, as I understand it, you are giving up a good law practice to spend your time in helping others—influencing their lives for good. Am I right?"

"Yes," I broke in.

He continued, "Well, that's what my life lacks, and that's what concerns me now. I've made money, myself, and I've helped a few others make it, too. But as I reflect on my life, I could count on my two hands the people whose lives I have really influenced for good, and I would have fingers to spare!"

As I left the bank that day I thought how empty and meaningless life would have been for me without the gospel and the Church. The most meaningful life that was ever lived was described by Peter as he spoke to Cornelius and his household, saying of Jesus, these simple words, that he "went about doing good, and healing all that were oppressed of the devil; for God was with him."[12]

I return to the premise that while the temple endowment and ordinances are required for eternal life, the sealing of the endowment and the ordinances upon us is no guarantee that eternal life will inevitably follow. To achieve that reward we must also be faithful in keeping our covenants and observing the laws and the commandments of God to the end of our lives.

Brigham Young has incisively pointed out that the right to say "This is my wife . . . here are my children" depends upon our keeping the commandments of God. He declared that "no man will have the privilege of gathering his [family—wife and children] around him [in the celestial glory] unless he proves himself worthy of them."[13]

Both God and man are involved in the temple covenants. It takes two to make them; it takes two to fulfill them. If man keeps his covenants, then God is bound to fulfill his promises, for he has said: "I, the Lord, am bound when ye do what I say; but when ye do not what I say, ye have no promise."[14]

One of the wisest of men, Solomon, emphasizes the importance of keeping the covenants we make with God in these words:

When thou vowest a vow unto God, defer not to pay it; for he hath no pleasure in fools: pay that which thou hast vowed.[15]

The receiving of the temple ordinances opens the gate and sets our course in the way of eternal life. The way is clear, and when a man has worthily made his covenants and received the ordinances he may know by the Spirit of God that he is "in the way." In the words of Isaiah, "And thine ears shall hear a word behind thee, saying, This is the way, walk ye in it."[16]

As we in worthiness receive the sacred temple ordinances and then follow "in the way," faithfully, unerringly observing the covenants we have made and the commandments of God, the seal of the "Holy Spirit of Promise, which the Father sheds forth upon all those who are just and true,"[17] may be placed upon our temple ordinances by the Holy Ghost, and our "calling and election" may "be made sure."

May we ponder with profit the inspired words of the great Book of Mormon King, Benjamin, as he concludes his final message to his people:

But this much I can tell you, that if ye do not watch yourselves, and your thoughts, and your words, and your deeds, and observe the commandments of God, and continue in the faith . . . even unto the end of your lives, ye must perish. And now, O man, remember, and perish not."[18]

Truly, we do not have anything "made" unless and until we "make it."

NOTES

1. D&C 130:20-21.
2. D&C 132:5.
3. *Journal of Discourses,* 17:116.
4. Matthew 10:22; see also 24:13.
5. D&C 78:7.
6. Stephen E. Whicher, ed., *Selections from Ralph Waldo Emerson,* 1960 ed. (Boston: Houghton Mifflin Co., 1957), p. 451.
7. Spencer W. Kimball, *The Miracle of Forgiveness* (Salt Lake City: Bookcraft, Inc. 1969), p. 237.
8. *Discourses of Brigham Young,* p. 196.
9. Matthew 6:33.
10. D&C 121:45-46.
11. D&C 121:34-35; italics added.
12. Acts 10:38.
13. *Journal of Discourses,* 17:116-19.
14. D&C 82:10.
15. Ecclesiastes 5:4.
16. Isaiah 30:21.
17. D&C 76:53.
18. Mosiah 4:30.

10

"WHO'S WHO" IN
THE ETERNAL WORLD

To be included in one of the Marquis Biographical Dictionaries, commonly known as *Who's Who*, is some evidence that the individual has attained a place of importance in the world, and often the individual takes great pride in having attained that place. While to be included in a "Who's Who" is not to be disparaged, it is, however, not necessarily the hallmark of greatness or goodness, particularly in the eyes of God.

In his perceptive essay entitled "Of Great Place," Lord Bacon writes:

> The rising unto place is laborious, and by pains men come to greater pains; and it is sometimes base; and by indignities men come to dignities. The standing is slippery, and the regress is either a downfall, or at least an eclipse, which is a melancholy thing. . . . *A place showeth the man.* And it showeth some to the better, and some to the worse.[1]

Speaking of place in the eternal world, the Master said to his disciples:

> In my Father's house are many mansions: if it were not so, I would have told you. I go to prepare a place for you.
>
> And if I go and prepare a place for you, I will come again, and receive you unto myself; that where I am, there ye may be also.[2]

Our conduct and choices in the premortal world and in this world unerringly, but justly and mercifully, determine our place in the eternal world. No mistakes will be made, no inequities will be involved.

In one of the greatest revelations ever given of God to man, an eternal "who's who" is set forth. It is an all-inclusive book; there is none to escape it; not one soul who has lived, or now lives, or who hereafter shall live, is left out. This heavenly "who's who" was revealed to the Prophet Joseph Smith and Sidney Rigdon in 1832 and soon became known as "the Vision," for it came by vision and revelation. It is prefaced with these words:

> We, Joseph Smith, Jun., and Sidney Rigdon, being in the Spirit on the sixteenth day of February, in the year of our Lord one thousand eight hundred and thirty-two—
>
> By the power of the Spirit our eyes were opened and our understandings were enlightened, so as to see and understand the things of God—
>
> Even those things which were from the beginning before the world was, which were ordained of the Father, through his Only Begotten Son, who was in the bosom of the Father, even from the beginning.[3]

And there followed a vision and understanding of the status of all men in the eternal world. The Prophet's own evaluation of this revelation is given to us in these words:

> Every law, every commandment, every promise, every truth, and every point touching the destiny of man, from Genesis to Revelation, where the purity of the scriptures remains unsullied by the folly of men, go to show the perfection of the theory [of different degrees of glory in the future life] and witnesses the fact that that document is a transcript from the records of the eternal world. The sublimity of the ideas; the purity of the language; the scope for action; the continued duration for completion, in order that the heirs of salvation may confess the Lord and bow the knee; the rewards for faithfulness, and the punishments for sins, are so much beyond the narrow-mindedness of men, that every honest man is constrained to exclaim: *"It came from God."*[4]

One such honest man—Charles W. Penrose—an early convert to the Church and later an apostle and counselor in the First Presidency, made this interesting appraisal of the vision:

He (God) gave to Joseph Smith and Sidney Rigdon, one of the most glorious visions that human beings ever gazed upon. It is the most complete and delightful that I have ever read. There is nothing in the book called the Bible that can compare with it. It is full of light; it is full of truth; it is full of glory; it is full of beauty. It portrays the future of all the inhabitants of the earth, dividing them into three grand classes or divisions—celestial, terrestrial, and telestial, or as compared to the glory of the sun, the glory of the moon, and the glory of the stars. It shows who will be redeemed, and what redemption they will enjoy; and describes the position the inhabitants of the earth will occupy when they enter into their future state.[5]

If, as the scriptures clearly attest, all men will be judged by their works,[6] and if judgment necessarily implies rewards and punishments, then, of necessity, we must accept the concept of a graded heaven, since rewards must differ even as men's works differ.

The Apostle Paul wrote of a man (undoubtedly referring to himself) who was "caught up to the third heaven."[7] What Paul meant by "the third heaven" is not clear from the text. Whether he referred to the celestial kingdom, or to a third heaven within that kingdom, he does not explain. That there is a third heaven in the celestial kingdom God revealed to the Prophet Joseph Smith.

One thing is certain in Paul's writings and that is that heaven is a graded place and that there are many glories or degrees of glory in it, for he writes:

> There is one glory of the sun, and another glory of the moon, and another glory of the stars: for one star differeth from another star in glory.
> So also is the resurrection of the dead.[8]

Paul associates the three glories—the glory of the sun, the glory of the moon and the glory of the stars—with the nature and kinds of bodies men will receive in the resurrection. The celestial body is likened unto the sun, the terrestrial body likened unto the moon, and other bodies (not named) likened unto the stars.[9] These latter bodies are identified in the vision received by Joseph Smith as "telestial" bodies.[10]

Parenthetically, it is now well known that certain of the stars are far more brilliant and glorious and are much larger than the moon or the sun in the firmament. It must, therefore, be understood that both Joseph Smith and Paul, in referring to the stars as being inferior to the moon and the sun in glory, are describing these heavenly bodies as they appear in glory to man on earth rather than their glory in reality.

Neither the Apostle Paul, nor any other biblical writer, details, or even outlines, the requirements for attaining to either of the three divisions in heaven. For this knowledge we must look to modern revelation and particularly to the revelation referred to as the Vision.

The basic requirements for attaining the celestial kingdom are set forth in that revelation as follows:

> These are they who received the testimony of Jesus, and believed on his name and were baptized after the manner of his burial, being buried in the water in his name, and this according to the commandment which he has given—
>
> That by keeping the commandments they might be washed and cleansed from all their sins, and receive the Holy Spirit by the laying on of the hands of him who is ordained and sealed unto this power;
>
> And who overcome by faith, and are sealed by the Holy Spirit of promise, which the Father sheds forth upon all those who are just and true.[11]

You will note that first among the celestial requirements is that we receive "the testimony of Jesus." What is this "testimony of Jesus"? John, the beloved disciple of the Master, tells us that "the testimony of Jesus is the spirit of prophecy."[12] This is helpful only if we understand the meaning of "the spirit of prophecy." The chief Apostle, Peter, gives us an explanation of "the spirit of prophecy" in his second epistle, where he says, "For the prophecy came not in old time by the will of man: but holy men of God spake as they were moved upon by the Holy Ghost."[13]

The Holy Ghost, then, is the "spirit of prophecy"—the Spirit by which prophecy is made possible—and it is by the Holy Ghost that man is given "the testimony of Jesus." It has been the right and mission of the Holy Ghost from the beginning to bear "record of the Father, and the Son."[14] The Apostle Paul attests to the truth of the words of Peter and John when he declares that "no man can say that Jesus is the Lord, but by the Holy Ghost."[15]

According to the revelation, the Holy Ghost is bestowed upon us by the laying on of the hands of a duly appointed and ordained servant of God, following faith, repentance, and baptism. Consequently, no one who has reached the age of accountability shall enter the celestial kingdom except he meet the requirements of faith in Jesus Christ, repentance of all transgressions, baptism "after the manner of Christ's burial," and the receiving of the Holy Ghost. The observance of these first requirements, and faithful adherence to his baptismal covenants, will open the gate and admit man to the celestial kingdom.

Admission to the celestial kingdom, great and glorious beyond our present comprehension though it be, is not the highest attainment possible to man. As has already been stated, the Lord revealed to Joseph Smith that within the celestial kingdom or glory there are three heavens or degrees of glory. To attain the highest of these—"the third heaven"—and obtain the fulness of all "the Father has to give," man must fully keep God's commandments and enter into and receive a fulness of the covenants and ordinances provided by God for the exaltation of his children, including, particularly, the ordinance of celestial marriage.

In the Vision the requirements for exaltation in the celestial kingdom are so interwoven with the blessings of exaltation that they are inextricably connected. It is a matter of inevitable cause and effect. In the words of Emerson, "Cause and effect are two sides of one fact." In his incisive essay on "Compensation," Emerson writes, "Every secret is told, every crime is punished, every virtue is rewarded, every wrong redressed, in silence and certainty. . . . Cause and effect, means and ends, seed and fruit, cannot be severed; for the effect already blooms in the cause, the end pre-exists in the means, the fruit in the seed."[16]

The Lord declares of those who are exalted in the celestial kingdom: "They are they who are the church of the Firstborn. They are they into whose hands the Father has given all things."[17] Therefore, to obtain all things of the Father, man will and must belong to the church of the Firstborn. To have membership in the church of the Firstborn is both a requirement and a blessing.

Since the designation "the Firstborn" is one of the titles applied to Jesus, it might be assumed that all who are members of The Church of Jesus Christ of Latter-day Saints, together with those who were members of the Church of Jesus Christ in former dispensations are, because of that membership, members of "the church of the Firstborn." Now, this is not a reality. There is no "church of the Firstborn" in the lesser kingdoms—telestial and terrestrial—but Latter-day Saints may have a substantial representation in these kingdoms. In the eternal world, membership in the "church of the Firstborn" is limited to those who, through their faith and devotion, have received and obeyed all the saving and exalting laws and ordinances of the gospel. "They are they who are priests and kings, who have received of his [the Father's] fulness, and of his glory; [who] are priests of the Most High, after the order of . . . the Only Begotten Son,"[18] and are "heirs of God and joint-heirs with [Jesus] Christ,"[19] who dwell in the presence of the Father and the Son and who, as shown in the heavenly vision, "are gods, even the sons of God."[20]

That man, by complete submission and obedience to the will and laws of God, may so progress in righteousness as to ultimately become like unto God and receive "of his [the Father's] fulness, and of his glory," is the clear and unmistakable import of this revelation. When a man attains this status, the kingly and priestly powers will merge and vest in him, and he will become and be both king and priest in his own kingdom. All of his blessings will be shared by the exalted companion who is sealed to him in the eternal marriage relationship, who will stand beside him as a queen and priestess. As is indicated in Doctrine and Covenants, section 121, he will govern and be governed by the power, principles and "doctrine of the priesthood." His scepter shall be "an unchanging scepter of righteousness and truth," and his dominion shall be magnified and shall be "an everlasting dominion, and without compulsory means it shall flow unto [him] forever and ever."

The titles "King of kings" and "Lord of lords,"[21] as applied to Christ in the scriptures and immortalized in Handel's world-acclaimed oratorio—the *Messiah*—are titles not limited in their application to his kingship and lordship over the kings and the mighty of this world, but more specifically refer to his position of supremacy over the kings and lords of the celestial world.

The concept that those who attain exaltation in the celestial kingdom may, in their endless progression, become "perfect," even as their "Father which is in heaven is perfect," and literally become "gods," is a shocking concept to the world and appears to approach blasphemy. Even to Latter-day Saints this may be a startling concept until we familiarize ourselves with what God has revealed in this dispensation concerning himself and his relationship to man. He has restored to us certain truths well known to the prophets of old. To Enoch, God revealed himself, saying, "Behold, I am God; Man of Holiness is my name."[22] Moses tells us that God spoke to Adam, saying,

> . . . teach it unto your children, that all men, everywhere, must repent, or they can in nowise inherit the kingdom of God, for no unclean thing can dwell there, or dwell in his presence; for . . . Man of Holiness is his name, and the name of his Only Begotten is the Son of Man, even Jesus Christ?[23]

The biblical references to Christ as the "Son of Man," therefore, are not references to any mortal lineage but to his lineage as the Son of God, he being, so far as the flesh is concerned, the Only Begotten of the Father—the "Man of Holiness."

The Latter-day Saint concept of God and man was put into a famous couplet by Lorenzo Snow shortly after his conversion to the gospel. A most interesting story of the origin of this couplet is related in the *Biography and Family Record of Lorenzo Snow*, as written and compiled by his sister, Eliza R. Snow Smith. Reared in a Baptist home, Lorenzo completed his scholastic training in Oberlin College, then an exclusively Presbyterian institution. He was then persuaded by his sister, Eliza, to join her in Kirtland, Ohio, and study Hebrew "under the tuition of an able Hebrew professor." Soon thereafter, Lorenzo became interested in Mormonism, joined the Church, and served several missions. Early in the spring of 1840 he was called on a mission to England.

Just a short time prior to his beginning the mission, Lorenzo Snow records a circumstance which, because of its sacredness, was "riveted" on his memory "never to be erased, so extraordinary was the manifestation." He was in the house of Elder H. G. Sherwood, who was "endeavoring to explain the parable of our Savior, when speaking of the husbandman who hired servants and sent them forth at different hours of the day to labor in his vineyard." President Snow later wrote:

> While attentively listening to his explanation, the Spirit of the Lord rested mightily upon me—the eyes of my under-standing were opened, and I saw as clear as the sun at noonday, with wonder and astonishment, the pathway of God and man. I formed the following couplet which expresses the revelation, as it was shown to me, . . .
>
> "As man now is, God once was:
> As God now is, man may be."[24]

The doctrinal concept expressed in the couplet had been revealed to the Prophet Joseph Smith and was taught by him prior to the formation of the couplet. So the stamp of truth was soon placed upon the inspired couplet.

We must not close the celestial "who's who" without reference to the promises made by the Lord to the righteous dead, who depart this life without the opportunity of receiving the gospel and its saving and exalting ordinances. Concerning a vision and revelation given to Joseph Smith in the Kirtland Temple on the twenty-first day of January, 1836, the Prophet writes:

> The heavens were opened upon us, and I beheld the celestial kingdom of God, and the glory thereof, whether in the body or out I cannot tell.
>
> I saw the transcendent beauty of the gate through which the heirs of that kingdom will enter, which was like unto circling flames of fire;

> Also the blazing throne of God, whereon was seated the Father and the Son.
>
> I saw the beautiful streets of that kingdom, which had the appearance of being paved with gold.
>
> I saw Father Adam and Abraham; and my father and my mother; my brother Alvin, that has long since slept;
>
> And marveled how it was that he had obtained an inheritance in that kingdom, seeing that he had departed this life before the Lord had set his hand to gather Israel the second time, and had not been baptized for the remission of sins.
>
> Thus came the voice of the Lord unto me, saying: All who have died without a knowledge of this gospel, who would have received it if they had been permitted to tarry, shall be heirs of the celestial kingdom of God;
>
> Also all that shall die henceforth without a knowledge of it, who would have received it with all their hearts, shall be heirs of that kingdom;
>
> For I, the Lord, will judge all men according to their works, according to the desire of their hearts.
>
> And I also beheld that all children who die before they arrive at the years of accountability are saved in the celestial kingdom of heaven.[25]

This vision should dispel forever the false but too prevalent notion that men and women can refuse, postpone, or defer acceptance of the gospel, with its saving and exalting ordinances, during this life and then, by accepting the gospel and receiving its ordinances after death, be entitled to the same rewards that are promised and assured those who accept and live the gospel fully in mortality.

It is manifested clearly from the revelation that only the dead who *had no opportunity* to receive the gospel in this life but "who would have received it with all their hearts" had the opportunity been afforded them, shall be entitled to salvation and exaltation in the celestial kingdom. The Church has erroneously been referred to as the "Church of the Second Chance." Those who refuse the gospel in this life may have a second chance to receive it after death, as did the disobedient in the days of Noah. However, the reward of this deferred acceptance is limited to the terrestrial glory. There is no *second chance* for *first place* after death.

It is almost a daily occurrence for men and women to come to the temple to have the sacred sealing ordinance administered to unite them eternally with their deceased wives and husbands. In many cases the deceased seemingly had ample opportunity to receive the marriage ordinance in life but refused or neglected to accept or qualify for this blessing before death. Since temple presidents are not the judges of the dead, the sealing ordinances are performed without regard to the qualifications or worthiness of the dead to receive such ordinances. The efficacy of the ordinance is a matter to be determined by the Judge of all men, who knows their lives, their opportunities to hear and accept the gospel and its exalting ordinances, and who knows the desires and intents of their hearts and minds. He will unerringly determine their worthiness or lack of worthiness to receive the ordinance of celestial marriage after death.

It must not be assumed from the language of this revelation that the righteous dead who have departed this life without the opportunity of receiving the gospel of Jesus Christ will be saved and exalted in the celestial kingdom without accepting the gospel and receiving the required ordinances. Such an assumption is contrary to the plain intent of the scriptures. The gospel will be taught to and accepted by the righteous dead who, through no fault of their own, failed to hear and accept it in this life. And the required ordinances instituted of God for their salvation and exaltation will be performed for them and in their behalf, by proxy, in the temples of our Lord.

Since it is the work and glory of God to "bring to pass the . . . eternal life of man"—which is exaltation in the celestial kingdom—God has given only the commandments, laws, rites, and ordinances which, if fully observed, will accomplish that objective. The terrestrial and telestial kingdoms of heaven are inferior to the celestial kingdom and are of lesser glory. God has revealed to man no rites or ordinances for entrance into these lesser kingdoms; none is intended or required. The way to the terrestrial kingdom, as revealed or implied in Doctrine and Covenants 76, is failure to receive all that God offers to give us and failure to give and do all that is required of us for attainment of eternal life. I find in the vision no specified requirement for the terrestrial kingdom but to live an honorable life. Except for that, we get there by default—by sins of omission which are defined by the Apostle James in the words, "To him that knoweth to do good, and doeth it not, to him it is sin."[26] Inactive goodness may lead to the terrestrial glory but never to the celestial.

Those who find place in the terrestrial kingdom are the honorable men of the earth who fall into four main classes: (1) "they who died without law,"[27] but who (it must be assumed), unlike Alvin Smith, would have failed to receive the law "with all their hearts" had the opportunity been given them; (2) they who were offered the gospel and the "testimony of Jesus" in this life and rejected it, but after death changed their minds and received it;[28] (3) they who were honorable but did not accept the gospel in life because they permitted themselves to be "blinded by the craftiness of men,"[29] but who could (it must be assumed) have found and understood the truth had they sought it earnestly; and (4) "they who are not valiant in the testimony of Jesus."[30]

This last classification is the one that should give Latter-day Saints grave cause for concern, for it is they who, in compliance with the first principles and ordinances of the gospel, have been baptized into The Church of Jesus Christ and have received "the testimony of Jesus." The Lord has made it very clear that Latter-day Saints who are not valiant must settle for less than the celestial kingdom and will forfeit all right to dwell in the presence of the Father in the eternal world. I repeat, inactive goodness is not the pathway to the celestial kingdom. It may lead to the terrestrial kingdom, but that is the end of the road.

I am reminded of the story I once heard told by the mayor of a large midwestern city. The first edition of the morning newspaper was about to go to press when word reached the newspaper offices that a wealthy woman, who occupied a prominent place in the social circles of the city, had died. It seemed imperative that notice of her death and some tribute to her appear in at least one issue of the morning newspaper. However, the writers on the staff to whom such assignments were customarily given had all completed their work and had long since left the offices of the paper.

A hasty survey of the remaining staff was made, and the only news reporter available was a sports writer. He got the unwelcome assignment. He was hard pressed to put together any story concerning the deceased lady. Neither he nor anyone else on the late night staff knew anything really good or evil about her. The newspaper files were not very helpful either. She belonged to several rather exclusive clubs, was in the upper, upper echelon of society, and had money to burn. But no one knew of anything really good or really bad to credit or charge her with.

Well, the sports writer wrote of her prominence in social circles and of her family connections, but to write a fitting tribute to her was his problem. He finally decided to pay her a tribute in verse and used the language he knew best—the vernacular of the sports world. The tribute read:

> Amy was not afraid to die;
> For her death knew no terrors;
> She came to bat a hundred times—
> No hits, no runs, no errors.

In Mormon philosophy, goodness is never self-contained, and failure to hit when a *hit* is possible and is expected of us is an *error, a serious error.*

Last and lowest among the heavenly kingdoms described in the vision is the telestial kingdom. Though vastly inferior to the higher kingdoms—terrestrial and celestial—nevertheless, as was shown to the Prophet, it "surpasses all understanding" in glory. This kingdom is not the "mansion"[31] which Jesus promised to prepare for his faithful followers, that they might be where he is. The inhabitants of the telestial glory are everlastingly deprived of the joy of living in the presence of the Father and the Son. Neither is this the kingdom prepared for the honorable men of the earth who failed to live the celestial law but who proved worthy of a terrestrial glory. The telestial kingdom will ultimately become the eternal home of those who on earth not only omitted to do what was required of them to attain a celestial or terrestrial kingdom, but who were also guilty of flagrant violations of the commandments of God, who were guilty of serious sins of commission.

These are they who . . . received not the gospel, neither the testimony of Jesus, neither the prophets, neither the everlasting covenant.

These are they who are liars, and sorcerers, and adulterers, and whoremongers, and whosoever loves and makes a lie.[32]

The Lord said of them that, after death, they shall be "cast down to hell and suffer the wrath of Almighty God, until the fulness of times, when Christ shall have subdued all enemies under his feet, and shall have perfected his work."[33]

One of the greatest of the Book of Mormon prophets, Alma, gives us a vivid description of that hell into which the wicked are thrust after death and of the wrath of God which shall come upon them. He writes:

There is a time appointed unto men that they shall rise from the dead; and there is a space between the time of death and the resurrection. And now, concerning this space of time, what becometh of the souls of men is the thing which I have inquired diligently of the Lord to know; and this is the thing which I *do know*. . . .

Now, concerning the state of the soul between death and the resurrection—Behold, it has been made known unto me by an angel, that the spirits of all men, as soon as they are departed from this mortal body . . . are taken home to that God who gave them life. . . .

And then shall it come to pass, that the spirits of the wicked, yea, who are evil—for behold, they have no part nor portion of the Spirit of the Lord; for behold, they chose evil works rather than good; therefore the spirit of the devil did enter into them, and take possession of their house—and these shall be cast out into outer darkness; there shall be weeping, and wailing, and gnashing of teeth, and this because of their own iniquity, being led captive by the will of the devil.

Now this is the state of the souls of the wicked, yea, in darkness, and a state of awful, fearful looking for the fiery indignation of the wrath of God upon them; thus they remain in this state . . . until the time of their resurrection.[34]

This fiery remorse of conscience and sense of guilt, which is hell, is described by another prophet in descriptive language, saying:

They are consigned to an awful view of their own guilt and abominations, which doth cause them to shrink from the presence of the Lord into a state of misery and endless torment.[35]

They of the telestial kingdom have chosen the longest road to resurrection and ultimate salvation, for they shall not be resurrected until after the millennial reign of Christ and after the "little season" that shall follow. While their bodies "sleep in the grave," their spirits suffer a sense of guilt and remorse which is as a quenchless fire and is called "hell." God does not consign the wicked to this hell because he takes delight in punishing his children. He grieves over their wickedness and does not delight in their punishment. The punishment of the wicked is a merciful punishment which, "like a refiner's fire, and like fullers' soap"[36] brings to pass repentance and a cleansing from sin.

Hell is a blessing to those whose conduct warrants such punishment. When they have repented; when they have bowed the knee and confessed that Jesus is the Christ; when they have ceased their wickedness and no more are liars, sorcerers, adulterers, whoremongers, and are no more numbered among those who love and make a lie, the mercy of God shall have claim upon them and they shall come forth in the final resurrection to a place in the telestial kingdom (provided they have not committed the unpardonable sin— the "sin against the Holy Ghost").[37]

In the telestial kingdom they shall enjoy a limited salvation. In the vision the Prophet saw that the inhabitants of the telestial world shall be heirs of salvation and "servants of the Most High; but where God and Christ dwell they cannot come, worlds without end."[38]

The last-quoted scripture is authority for the fact that, while we believe in the principle of eternal progression, there is no passing from kingdom to kingdom in the eternal world. Why is this so? In the first place, eternal progression applies to all the heavenly kingdoms. Therefore, since those who are in the celestial kingdom shall progress and, possibly, at a faster pace than those in the lower kingdoms, how shall those in the lower kingdoms overtake them?

There is another and probably more important reason. God has revealed that celestial, terrestrial, and telestial bodies are different in the resurrection; that such is the nature of a telestial body that it can abide the glory of a telestial kingdom but cannot abide the glory of a terrestrial kingdom. And so, likewise, they who possess bodies of a terrestrial nature cannot endure the glory of the celestial kingdom.

This is explained in the revelation given by the Lord through Joseph Smith at Kirtland, Ohio, on December 27, 1832. The Prophet communicated this revelation to the Saints in Missouri by letter addressed to William W. Phelps. So important and beautiful is the revelation that the Prophet begins the letter with these words: "I send you the 'olive leaf' which we have plucked from the Tree of Paradise, the Lord's message of peace to us."[39] In this revelation the Lord declared:

> For he who is not able to abide the law of a celestial kingdom cannot abide a celestial glory.
> And he who cannot abide the law of a terrestrial kingdom cannot abide a terrestrial glory.
> And he who cannot abide the law of a telestial kingdom cannot abide a telestial glory; therefore he is not meet for a kingdom of glory. Therefore he must abide a kingdom which is not a kingdom of glory.[40]

Apostle Melvin J. Ballard, in an address delivered in the Ogden Tabernacle on September 22, 1922, put it this way:

> The very fibre and texture of the celestial body is more pure and holy than a telestial or terrestrial body, and a celestial body alone can endure celestial glory.[41]

The Lord further explains that if, in this life, we have complied with the laws and commandments and ordinances entitling us to a place in the celestial kingdom, we shall, in the resurrection, receive our bodies quickened by a portion of celestial glory. He said:

> They who are of a celestial spirit shall receive the same body which was a natural body; . . . and your glory shall be that glory by which your bodies are quickened.
> Ye who are quickened by a portion of the celestial glory shall then receive of the same, even a fulness.
> And they who are quickened by a portion of the terres-

trial glory shall then receive of the same, even a fulness.

And also they who are quickened by a portion of the telestial glory shall then receive of the same, even a fulness.[42]

Thus it is that in the resurrection the nature and constitution of our bodies will be determined by the law we have lived, whether it be the celestial law, the terrestrial law, or the telestial law. And we shall have place in the celestial, the terrestrial, or the telestial kingdom according to the glory with which our bodies are quickened and may go on to receive a fulness of that glory. But there is no passing from kingdom to kingdom.

Since by obedience to law we choose our kingdom and glory, may we right now choose wisely the kingdom and glory we would have in the eternal world, and then live for it. There is but one way to exaltation in the celestial kingdom, only one way to eternal life, and that is to observe and keep the commandments of God and receive the ordinances of his holy house in their fulness.

If we fail to have our names written in the celestial heaven, where God and Christ dwell, it will be by our own choice and conduct; it will be the result of unwise priorities established in our lives; it will be our responsibility and ours alone. What sorrow such failure would bring! How deep the bitterness in the familiar lines:

> Of all sad words of tongue or pen,
> The saddest are these: "It might have been."

As Latter-day Saints—

If we believe what God has revealed—
If we trust his promises—
If we accept his offer—
If we aspire to receive *all* that the Father has to give—
We will and must pass

THROUGH TEMPLE DOORS.

NOTES

1. Sir Francis Bacon in *The Harvard Classics* (*Bacon, Milton's Prose, Thos. Browne*) New York: P.F. Collier & Son., 1909), 3:28-30.
2. John 14:2-3.
3. D&C 76:11-13.
4. *History of the Church,* 1:252-253.
5. *Journal of Discourses,* 24:92.
6. Revelation 20:12-13.
7. 2 Corinthians 12:2.
8. 1 Corinthians 15:41-42.
9. 1 Corinthians 15:40-41.
10. D&C 76:81.
11. D&C 76:51-53.
12. Revelation 19:10.
13. 2 Peter 1:21.
14. Moses 6:66.
15. 1 Corinthians 12:3.
16. Ralph Waldo Emerson, "Compensation," *The Complete Writings of Ralph Waldo Emerson* (New York: Wm. H. Wise and Co., 1929).
17. D&C 76:54-55.
18. D&C 76:56-57.
19. Romans 8:17.
20. D&C 76:58.
21. 1 Timothy 6:15; see also Revelation 19:16.
22. Moses 7:35.
23. Moses 6:57.
24. Eliza Roxy Snow Smith, *Biography and Family Record of Lorenzo Snow* (Salt Lake City: Deseret News Co., 1884), p. 46.
25. Joseph Smith—Vision of the Celestial Kingdom 1:1-10.
26. James 4:17.
27. D&C 76:72.
28. D&C 76:74.
29. D&C 76:75.
30. D&C 76:79.
31. John 14:2-3.
32. D&C 76:100-101, 103.
33. D&C 76:106.
34. Alma 40:9, 11, 13-14; italics added.
35. Mosiah 3:25.
36. D&C 128:24; Malachi 3:3.
37. D&C 76:83.
38. D&C 76:43-44, 112.
39. *History of the Church,* 1:316.
40. D&C 88:22-24.
41. Melvin J. Ballard, *The Three Degrees of Glory* (Salt Lake City: Deseret Book Co., 1965), p. 30.
42. D&C 88:28-31.

INDEX

Index

Book designed by Bailey-Montague and Associates
Composed by Type Design
in Palatino with display lines in Palatino Italic
Printed by Publishers Press
on Bookcraft Publishers Antique
Bound by Mountain States Bindery
in Kivar 5, Shasta White, Morocco Grain